·WITH·WARMEST·REGARDS·

A·CELEBRATION·OF
OUR·CUSTOMERS'·RECIPES·AND·TRADITIONS

DAYTON'S  HUDSON'S

·ILLUSTRATIONS·BY·TOMIE dePAOLA·

CONTEMPORARY
BOOKS
A TRIBUNE NEW MEDIA COMPANY

Interior design by Kim Bartko

FRANGO is a registered trademark of Dayton Hudson Corporation.

Published by Contemporary Books, Inc.
Two Prudential Plaza, Chicago, Illinois 60601-6790
Manufactured in the United States of America
International Standard Book Number: 0-8092-3214-6
10   9   8   7   6   5   4   3   2   1

DEDICATED TO OUR CUSTOMERS

AND OUR COMMUNITIES.

Contents

INTRODUCTION

Over the years our friends, customers, and communities have shared some very special traditions with Dayton's, Marshall Field's, and Hudson's—our family of stores. Delicious food, freshly prepared and beautifully served, is one of those traditions. Since the opening of our very first tearoom in 1890, many of our customers have made our restaurants and recipes part of their family traditions and celebrations.

Good times are for sharing, and in 1989 we were very happy to share our employees' own favorite recipes in our first cookbook, *Potluck for 24,000*. This book, all net profits of which are donated to local United Way agencies, has been so popular with our customers (we've since expanded it to include even more recipes and changed the name to *Potluck for 33,000*) that in 1992 we served up *Someone's in the Kitchen with Dayton's, Marshall Field's, and Hudson's*, a tempting collection of the most popular recipes from our own bakeries, kitchens, and restaurants. Sharing our recipes was our way of saying "thank you" for making us feel like a friend to you and your families.

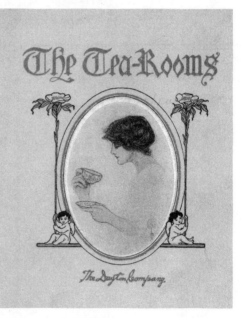

Now, to return the favor, we are delighted to present *With Warmest Regards*, a brand-new collection of delectable, easy-to-make recipes from you—our customers. We've put your favorite original recipes together in one book so that all of our friends and neighbors can enjoy them. From appetizers, soups, and salads to main courses, side dishes, and, of course, desserts, each recipe offers mouthwatering proof that our customers love creating great-tasting meals, snacks, and treats just as much as we do.

There's another reason why this cookbook is important to us. It continues a very important tradition we share with you—community involvement. At Dayton's, Marshall Field's, and Hudson's, we count on the strength and vitality of the communities in which we do business. And we know that individuals, families, and communities count on stores like ours to help foster happy, healthy neighborhoods through corporate giving. In 1946 our company became a founding member of the "Five Percent Club," a landmark movement encouraging corporations to commit five percent of federally taxable income to support community nonprofit organizations. Since then, we have contributed more than $300 million to social action and arts programs across America. By giving a portion of each dollar our customers spend in our stores back to the communities where we all live—more than any other major retailer—we continue that spirit of "five percent" to this day.

How do our contributions help communities? We give where we believe it will make a difference. We're making an investment in the future of our youth, providing support to give children a positive start in life. We support the arts, social action, and volunteerism in a number of ways, including local grants and our employee volunteer program.

Another way we support our neighborhoods is through donations to United Way. In 1994 we were one of the largest contributors nationally to United Way organizations. We'd like to do even more—and that's where this book can make a real difference. We like to think of *With Warmest Regards* as a true community project—and for that reason, we are donating all net profits from the sale of this cookbook to United Way. The net profits from your purchase of each book will go right back into our communities, making the cities and neighborhoods we share safer, better places to live and raise our children.

In many ways, we all gain as much as we give. The result of our—and your—service to our communities enables everyone to look forward to a brighter, more enriched future. We at Dayton's, Marshall Field's, and Hudson's are happy to be able to share this cookbook with you, and to share your remarkable sense of community participation and spirit.

Thank you, and enjoy!

About Tomie dePaola

Tomie dePaola was born on September 15, 1934, in Meriden, Connecticut. Since 1956 his career has been as a professional artist and designer, a teacher of art, a painter and muralist, and an artist and author of books for children. He has illustrated almost two hundred books and has written the stories for one-third of them.

Tomie has designed greeting cards, posters, magazine and catalog covers, record album covers, and theater and nightclub sets. Many of his paintings and murals were created for churches and monasteries in New England. His work has been exhibited in many one-person shows and group shows, including exhibitions at The Cedar Rapids Museum of Art (Cedar Rapids, Iowa), The Museum of Fine Art (Houston, Texas), The Art Institute of Chicago (Chicago, Illinois), and the Dayton Art Institute (Dayton, Ohio).

Tomie, who is perhaps best known for his works for children, is creative director of Whitebird Books, his own publishing imprint at The Putnam & Grosset Group in New York City. With more than five million copies in print, his books have been published in more than fifteen different countries, and he has received virtually every significant recognition for his works, including the Caldecott Honor Award, the Kerlan Award, and the Regina Medal. In 1990 he was the sole U.S. nominee in illustration for the prestigious international award the Hans Christian Andersen Medal, and he received the Smithson Medal from the Smithsonian Institution.

Tomie dePaola lives in New London, New Hampshire. We at Dayton's, Marshall Field's, and Hudson's are extremely honored to feature Tomie's illustrations, created especially for this book, in *With Warmest Regards*; and we are delighted at, but not in the least surprised by, his warmth and generosity in contributing to this community project.

MEXICAN PINWHEELS

MAREEN L. ROACH • DAYTON'S

"My husband is absolutely crazy about this recipe. He's even eaten these as burritos because he couldn't wait for them to be sliced into appetizer-sized portions."

1 8-ounce package cream cheese, at room temperature
1 8-ounce container sour cream
½ teaspoon seasoned salt
¼ teaspoon garlic powder
1 4-ounce can chopped green chilies, drained
½ cup thinly sliced scallions (stems included)
½ cup sliced pitted black olives
5 10-inch flour tortillas
1½ cups (about 12 ounces) prepared salsa

1. In a mixing bowl, blend together cream cheese, sour cream, salt, and garlic powder. Mix until smooth.

2. Fold chilies, scallions, and olives into mixture. Mix gently and thoroughly.

3. Spread equal amounts of mixture onto each tortilla, beginning at one edge of the tortilla. Leave about one-fourth of each tortilla uncovered.

4. Roll each tortilla toward the section that is not covered with mixture. Wrap each separately in plastic wrap and refrigerate for 1 hour.

5. Remove and discard plastic wrap. Slice each burrito into 8 rounds. Serve with salsa on the side.

Serves 10 to 20

COOK'S NOTES

OLIVADA CROSTINI

ST. PAUL MAYOR NORM COLEMAN
AND LAURIE COLEMAN • DAYTON'S

"This elegant yet easy-to-make appetizer is perfect for almost any occasion."

2 6-ounce cans pitted whole black olives, drained
3 tablespoons olive oil
2 tablespoons pine nuts, toasted (see Note)
2 large cloves garlic
Salt and black pepper to taste
1 ½-pound French baguette
1 7-ounce jar roasted red bell peppers, drained and sliced thin
4 to 5 ounces goat cheese

1. Preheat oven to 350°F.

2. In a food processor, combine olives, oil, pine nuts, and garlic. Process until chopped fine. Season with salt and pepper.

3. Slice baguette on the diagonal into 28 ½-inch slices. Arrange in a single layer on a baking sheet. Bake until lightly toasted around the edges (about 10 minutes).

4. Spread 1 tablespoon olive mixture on each toast slice. Top with bell peppers and cheese. Add pepper to taste and serve.

Serves 6 to 8

NOTE

To toast pine nuts, place in a non-stick skillet over medium heat, and stir frequently until nuts are lightly browned (2 to 3 minutes). Do not burn.

OH-LA-LA MUSHROOMS

STEPHANIE NANKERVIS • HUDSON'S

"These marinated mushrooms are favorite fare at holiday gatherings and at any party."

1 pound (about 4 cups) fresh mushrooms
⅔ cup tarragon vinegar
½ cup extra-virgin olive oil
2 teaspoons water
Dash hot sauce
1½ teaspoons salt
1 whole clove, crushed
Dash black pepper
1 medium red or white onion, sliced thin
1 tablespoon chopped fresh parsley

1. Clean mushrooms. Slice each in half and set aside.

2. In a large bowl, combine all remaining ingredients. Add mushrooms and stir to coat. Cover bowl and refrigerate for 6 to 12 hours, stirring occasionally.

3. Before serving, drain mushrooms, discarding excess marinade. Transfer to a serving platter and serve with party toothpicks.

Serves 8

COOK'S NOTES

CRABMEAT au GRATIN

ROSE E. SNIDER • HUDSON'S

"We entertain a lot, and this always wins accolades from our guests. If you'd like, you can substitute lobster for the crab."

> 2 tablespoons butter, melted
> 1 cup dry bread crumbs
> 1 10¾-ounce can condensed cream of celery soup
> ¼ cup water
> 1 tablespoon dry white wine, if desired
> 2 6-ounce cans lump crabmeat, drained and picked over
> 1 tablespoon minced fresh parsley
> ½ cup (about 2 ounces) shredded sharp cheddar cheese

1. Preheat the oven to 400°F.

2. In a mixing bowl, pour butter over bread crumbs. Toss to coat. Set aside.

3. In a separate mixing bowl, combine soup, water, and, if desired, wine. Add crabmeat and parsley and mix well.

4. Place ⅔ cup crabmeat mixture into each of six 6-ounce gratin dishes. Top each with equal amounts of cheese and bread crumb mixture. Bake for 20 minutes, until casseroles are bubbly and bread crumb mixture is golden brown.

Serves 6

CREAMY CRAB AND CRISPS

LAURIE ANN REDLOWSK • HUDSON'S

"This appetizer always seems to appeal to people who have an insatiable appetite for excitement and amusement. I've served it abroad, in the tropics, at work to my staff, and at home to my neighbors to enjoy with beer and baseball. It is always received with rave reviews."

16 to 24 imitation crab legs, chopped and shredded
1 pound cheddar cheese, shredded (about 4 cups)
1 medium onion, chopped fine
2 tablespoons lemon juice
1 cup mayonnaise-style salad dressing
Salt and black pepper to taste
Crisp crackers

1. In a mixing bowl, blend together all ingredients except crackers.
2. To serve, spread mixture onto crackers or place mixture in a serving bowl and serve with crackers on the side.

Serves 8 to 10

COOK'S NOTES

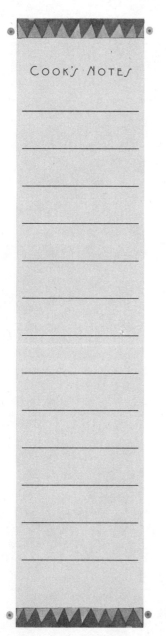

MINI-PASTIES WITH SWEET PICANTE SAUCE

MARIE RIZZIO • HUDSON'S

"For almost twenty years our family lived in the Upper Peninsula of Michigan, where the Pastie is quite popular. Miners used to bring these hearty meat pies from home for lunch. The original Pastie was made with a pie dough of suet, lard, or shortening. This modified version calls for refrigerated biscuit dough."

MINI-PASTIES

    1 large egg
    1 tablespoon water
    5 ounces ground turkey
    1 small red potato, peeled and diced
    ⅓ cup chopped onion
    ¼ shredded rutabaga or carrot
    1 tablespoon snipped fresh parsley
    ½ teaspoon salt
    ¼ teaspoon black pepper
    ¼ teaspoon garlic powder
    1 10-ounce can refrigerated buttermilk biscuits (10 biscuits)
    2 ounces cheddar cheese, shredded (about ½ cup)
    Garnish: parsley sprigs

SWEET PICANTE SAUCE

    ¼ cup prepared picante sauce
    ¼ cup ketchup

1. Preheat oven to 400°F.

2. Make the Pasties. In a small bowl, beat egg and water together. Set aside.

3. In a medium skillet, brown turkey over medium heat (5 to 7 minutes). Stir in potato, onion, rutabaga or carrot, parsley, salt, pepper, and garlic powder. Reduce heat to low, cover, and cook for 10 to 15 minutes more, until potato is fork-tender.

4. Separate biscuits into halves. Roll or press each half into a 4-inch circle. Place equal amounts of turkey mixture on one side of each biscuit half. Sprinkle with cheese.

5. Fold over each biscuit half to cover mixture and form a semicircle. Crimp edges together to seal. Using a fork, lightly prick each Pastie twice.

6. Place Pasties on a cookie sheet that has been lightly sprayed with vegetable oil spray, and brush tops with egg-water mixture. Bake for 8 to 10 minutes, until golden.

7. Make the sauce. In a small bowl, combine picante sauce and ketchup. Mix thoroughly.

8. To serve, place Pasties on a serving platter and garnish with parsley sprigs. Serve sauce hot or cold on the side.

Serves 10

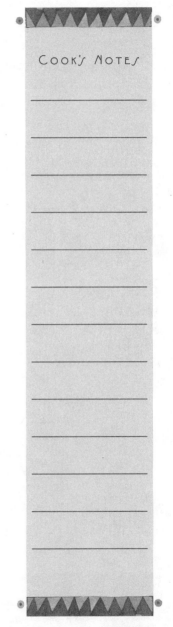

COOK'S NOTES

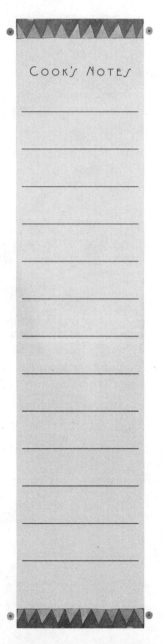

LOW-CAL, LOW-FAT TORTILLA ROLL-UPS

ROSALYN H. PACHTER • MARSHALL FIELD'S

*"I created this appetizer for a dinner party that included several guests who had
health concerns. I wanted to offer them a delicious, heart-healthy appetizer,
and this was perfect. Many people liked it so much, they asked for the recipe."*

> 1 8-ounce jar prepared honey mustard
> 8 8-inch flour tortillas
> 8 large leaves red leaf lettuce
> 1 pound smoked turkey, sliced thin
> 3 medium carrots, shredded

1. Spread 2 tablespoons honey mustard on each tortilla, leaving a ½-inch
   border all around the tortilla. Top each with 1 leaf lettuce, 2 slices
   turkey, and 2 tablespoons carrot.
2. Roll each tortilla into a burrito. Wrap each in plastic wrap and refrigerate for several hours (or overnight).
3. When ready to serve, remove and discard plastic wrap from tortillas.
   Cut each into 1-inch pieces and serve.

Serves 16 to 20

STUFFED MUSHROOMS

MARLENE A. KONSDORF • HUDSON'S

"I enjoy making these special treats at Christmastime, and my family loves to scoop them up right from the baking sheet, fresh and warm from the oven."

> 20 large fresh mushrooms
> 1½ pounds bulk sausage
> 1 medium onion, diced
> 2 slices white or whole-wheat bread, crumbed (see Note)
> ⅛ teaspoon dried thyme
> ½ pound mozzarella cheese, shredded (about 2 cups)

1. Preheat oven to 350°F.

2. Clean and stem mushrooms. Finely chop stems. Set aside mushroom caps and stem pieces.

3. Brown sausage in a skillet over medium heat (about 5 to 7 minutes). Drain on paper toweling.

4. Place sausage, onion, mushroom stem pieces, bread crumbs, and thyme in a large bowl. Mix thoroughly. Stir in cheese.

5. Stuff each mushroom cap with mixture and place on an ungreased cookie sheet. Bake for 15 to 20 minutes, until stuffing is lightly browned and cheese is melted. Serve warm.

Serves 10

NOTE

Tear up bread and place in food processor. Pulse until crumbs are formed.

COOK'S NOTES

AMANDA'S NORWEGIAN MEATBALLS

MRS. JEANE JENSON • HUDSON'S

"This recipe belonged to my mother, Amanda Arneson, and she used to prepare it for all the Norwegian holidays. Now, when the grandchildren come to our house, they always ask for 'Grandma's meatballs.'"

MEATBALLS

2½ pounds lean twice-ground beef (see Note)
½ pound lean twice-ground pork (see Note)
½ cup dry bread crumbs
3 large eggs, beaten
2 teaspoons sugar
2 teaspoons salt
½ teaspoon ground ginger
½ teaspoon ground nutmeg
½ teaspoon ground allspice
¼ teaspoon black pepper
½ cup chopped onion
3 tablespoons cornstarch
1 cup milk
¼ cup vegetable oil

GRAVY

3 tablespoons vegetable shortening
3 tablespoons all-purpose flour
1 quart beef broth
½ cup heavy cream, if desired

1. Preheat oven to 325°F.

2. Make the meatballs. In a large mixing bowl, combine ground meats, bread crumbs, eggs, sugar, salt, seasonings, and onion. In a small bowl, dissolve cornstarch in milk. Add to meat mixture and combine thoroughly. Shape the mixture into 1-inch balls.

3. In a large skillet, heat oil over medium heat. Fry meatballs in batches (do not crowd) until golden brown (about 5 minutes), turning occasionally to brown evenly. Drain on paper toweling and place in a single layer in a large casserole dish.

4. Make the gravy. Discard fat from the skillet. Wipe with a paper towel. Melt shortening in the skillet over medium-low heat. Stir in flour until blended. Add broth and continue to cook until mixture has thickened slightly (3 to 4 minutes). If desired, stir in cream.

5. Pour gravy over meatballs. Bake until hot and bubbly (about 30 minutes). Serve warm.

Serves 12 to 20

NOTE

Ask your butcher to grind the ground beef and ground pork one more time. This makes for a truly tender meatball.

COOK'S NOTES

COOK'S NOTES

DEEP-FRIED PORK WONTON

LANA LIE • HUDSON'S

"Everyone loves this homemade wonton appetizer, which I learned to make in Indonesia, my home. I usually serve a variety of appetizers at my parties, and these are always the first to be finished off."

> 1 pound ground pork
> 2 scallions, chopped fine
> 1 teaspoon finely chopped garlic
> ½ cup cooked baby shrimp, chopped fine
> ¼ teaspoon salt
> ¼ teaspoon black pepper
> 1 package wonton skins (96 skins)
> 2 to 3 cups canola or vegetable oil
> 2 to 3 cups prepared sweet and sour sauce

1. In a large bowl, combine pork, scallions, garlic, shrimp, salt, and pepper. Mix thoroughly.

2. Place 1 teaspoon of the mixture in the center of each wonton skin. To form the wontons, moisten the edge of each skin with water. Fold skin in half over mixture to form a triangle and crimp closed. Lift up the points at each end of the fold and pinch together.

3. Heat oil in a large frying pan or a wok over medium-high heat. Fry wontons in batches (do not crowd) until light golden brown, about 1 minute. Drain on paper toweling. Serve with sweet and sour sauce for dipping.

Serves 16 to 20

SWEET ITALIAN SAUSAGE APPETIZER

NANCY DARBUT • DAYTON'S

"Served with French bread, this is a hearty treat for parties and other get-togethers."

1 pound sweet or mild Italian sausage links
2 tablespoons olive oil or peanut oil
1 medium green bell pepper, sliced thin
1 medium yellow bell pepper, sliced thin
1 medium red bell pepper, sliced thin
1 large onion, sliced thin
2 cloves garlic, chopped
1 26-ounce jar prepared marinara sauce
1 cup dry white wine

1. Preheat oven to 300°F.

2. Place sausage in a large pot and cover with water. Bring to a boil over medium heat and continue boiling for 15 minutes. Drain in a colander. Puncture sausage with the tines of a fork. Set aside to cool.

3. Heat oil in a large sauté pan over medium heat. Add bell peppers, onion, and garlic and sauté until peppers are fork-tender (5 to 6 minutes). Do not overcook peppers. Remove pan from heat.

4. Cut sausage into bite-sized pieces. Using a knife, gently score each piece. Remove and discard skin. Place sausage in a 9″ × 13″ baking dish.

5. In a bowl, combine marinara sauce and white wine. Pour over sausage and top with peppers and onions. Cover dish and bake for 1 hour.

Serves 12 to 16

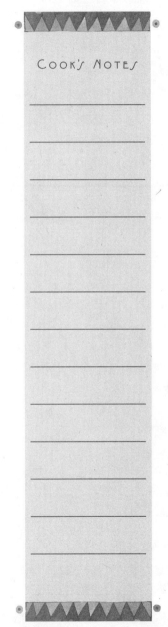

COOK'S NOTES

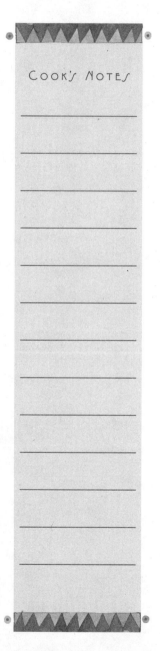

COOK'S NOTES

EASY CHOPPED LIVER

ESTELLE MAKROUER • HUDSON'S

"This recipe was used by my mother and is now a favorite of mine as well as of my two sisters, my daughters, and my nieces. Soon it will be handed down to my granddaughter, who is attending the University of Michigan."

½ cup butter or margarine
2 medium onions, chopped
1 pound chicken livers
3 large eggs, hard cooked
1 large sweet potato, boiled and peeled
1 teaspoon salt
Black pepper to taste
Crackers or matzo

1. In a large skillet, melt butter over medium heat. Add onions and cook until they begin to soften (4 to 5 minutes). Add chicken livers and cook until no longer pink (about 10 minutes).

2. Transfer liver mixture to a food processor. Add eggs, sweet potato, salt, and pepper and process until smooth. Adjust seasoning to taste and transfer to a serving bowl. Serve with crackers or matzo.

Serves 10 to 12

QUICK CHILI DIP

DONNA V. DUFFIELD • HUDSON'S

"This appetizer is easy to make, and it's a big hit at parties. It tastes terrific, even when made with low-fat substitutions for the cream cheese and cheddar cheese called for here."

1 8-ounce package cream cheese, at room temperature
1 8-ounce can prepared chili without beans
1 4-ounce can chopped green chilies, drained
1 medium onion, chopped, if desired
1 medium tomato, chopped, if desired
¾ pound cheddar cheese, shredded (about 3 cups)
½ cup chopped pitted black olives, if desired
Corn chips or tortilla chips

1. Preheat oven to 375°F.

2. Spread cream cheese evenly over bottom of an 8-inch square glass or ceramic dish. Spread chili evenly over cream cheese. Sprinkle chilies, and, if desired, onion and tomato over chili. Top with cheese and, if desired, olives.

3. Bake for 20 to 30 minutes or until cheese is bubbly. Serve with corn chips or tortilla chips.

Serves 6 to 8

VARIATION

Turkey chili may be substituted for beef chili. Light or low-fat cream cheese and cheddar cheese may be used. Taco-flavored cheese may be substituted for cheddar cheese.

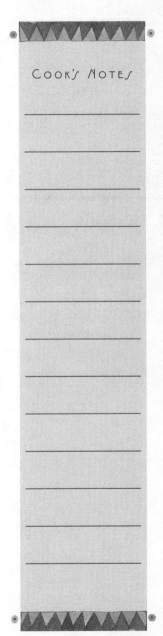

COOK'S NOTES

PECAN DIP

The Honorable Dennis Archer, Mayor, City of Detroit •
The Honorable Trudy Duncombe Archer, Judge,
36th District Court • Hudson's

"Served with tortilla chips, this is a delicious appetizer or snack. It's also great on a bagel."

Dip

> 2 8-ounce packages cream cheese, at room temperature
> 1 cup sour cream
> 5 ounces dried beef
> ½ cup chopped green bell pepper
> 1 small onion, chopped fine
> 1 teaspoon garlic salt
> ½ teaspoon black pepper

Topping

> ¼ cup butter
> 1 cup (6 ounces) chopped pecans
> Dash salt

1. Preheat oven to 350°F.

2. Make the dip. In a small mixing bowl, combine all ingredients for dip. Mix well. Spread evenly into a 9″ glass pie plate.

3. Make the topping. In a small skillet, melt butter over medium heat. Add pecans and salt. Mix thoroughly.

4. Pour topping over dip mixture and bake for 20 to 25 minutes.

Serves 8 to 12

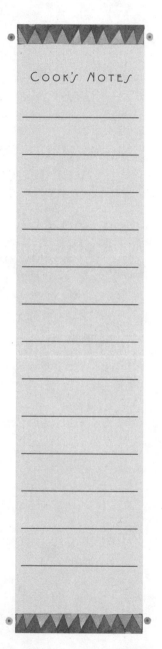

COOK'S NOTES

SASSY SOUTHWESTERN DIP

Elizabeth Forster • Dayton's

"This recipe is fresh, light, full of color, and easy to make. It's also a great way to use some of those cherry tomatoes that all seem to ripen at once. I love to bring this tasty dip to potlucks or when I'm visiting friends on hot afternoons."

1 medium onion
1 medium green bell pepper
1 pint cherry tomatoes
1 6-ounce can pitted black olives
Minced fresh garlic or garlic powder to taste
1 to 2 teaspoons vegetable oil, if desired
Hot sauce to taste, if desired
Chips, crackers, or raw vegetables for dipping

1. Coarsely chop onion, bell pepper, tomatoes, and olives. Place in a bowl and mix together with garlic or garlic powder and, if desired, oil. Add hot sauce, if desired, and stir. Let stand for at least 45 minutes before serving.

2. To serve, stir and transfer to a serving bowl. Serve with chips, crackers, or raw vegetables.

Serves 8 to 12

COOK'S NOTES

HONEY DIP FOR VEGGIES

JEANETTE ANDERSON • DAYTON'S

"Many years ago I worked with a great group of women. We'd regularly get together to enjoy potluck dinners and exchange recipes. Whenever I make this, I'm reminded of all the good times our group had."

1½ cups mayonnaise
7 drops hot sauce
2 tablespoons honey
2 tablespoons ketchup
2 tablespoons minced onion
2 tablespoons lemon juice
1 teaspoon curry powder
Assorted fresh vegetables, cut into bite-sized pieces

1. In a mixing bowl, combine all ingredients except fresh vegetables. Blend thoroughly and pour into a serving bowl. Serve with assorted fresh vegetables.

Serves 6 to 8

RICH MAN BUTLER SAUCE AND AVOCADOS

MARILYN SMITH • DAYTON'S

"This wonderful recipe was given to my husband by Chun Rim, a Korean secretary he employed when we lived in San Jose, California. She had received it from a friend who worked as a butler for a rich man—hence the name 'Rich Man Butler Sauce.'"

> ¼ cup ketchup
> ¼ cup Worcestershire sauce
> ¼ cup sugar
> ¼ cup butter
> 2 medium-sized ripe avocados

1. In a small saucepan, combine ketchup, Worcestershire sauce, sugar, and butter. Heat over medium-low heat until warm (do not boil).

2. Peel and halve avocados, discarding pits. Cut each half into 4 slices.

3. Place 4 slices avocado on each of 4 serving plates. Spoon warm sauce over avocado and serve immediately.

Serves 4

COOK'S NOTES

CRANBERRY TEA

PATTI McEACHRON • DAYTON'S

"This heavenly beverage is wonderful for fall or winter family gatherings. Children especially love it."

3 cups water
1 12-ounce bag cranberries
   (fresh or frozen)
2½ cups sugar
1 cup frozen orange juice
   concentrate

1 cup frozen lemonade concentrate
1 quart apple juice
12 drops liquid cloves (see Note)
10 drops liquid cinnamon (see Note)
2 tablespoons instant tea

1. In a medium pot, bring water to a boil. Add cranberries and boil until berries pop (about 3 minutes).
2. Drain and discard cranberries, reserving juice. Return juice to pot. Add all remaining ingredients and bring to a boil.
3. Remove from heat and let cool. Transfer to a storage jar or container. Syrup may be stored in the refrigerator for up to 3 weeks.
4. For each serving, mix ½ cup syrup with ¾ cup water. Heat and serve. This recipe yields about 10 cups syrup, to make up to 25 cups of tea.

Serves 25

NOTE

If liquid cloves and liquid cinnamon are not available, substitute 5 whole cloves and 2 cinnamon sticks. Break cinnamon sticks in halves, wrap cloves and cinnamon sticks in cheesecloth, and secure with string. Remove before storing syrup.

TOMATO BOUILLON

LESLIE WARD • HUDSON'S

"My mother often made this recipe, using fresh herbs from her garden. I can remember running off to pick the herbs, smelling the rich fragrance of the earth and gathering the oregano, basil, dill, and marjoram in my child-sized hands to add to this soup."

1 quart tomato juice
½ bay leaf
2 whole cloves
1¼ teaspoons dried oregano
½ teaspoon sugar
¼ teaspoon dried dill weed
¼ teaspoon dried basil
¼ teaspoon dried marjoram

1. Combine all ingredients in a bowl. Mix well. Cover and let stand at room temperature for 1 hour. Chill before serving.

Serves 8

COOK'S NOTES

MINESTRA CASALINGA

TINA CHIAPPA • MARSHALL FIELD'S

"This recipe was first prepared for me by my grandmother, and it soon became one of my favorite childhood dishes. Grandmother usually used leftover scraps of pasta from her homemade ravioli or tortellini. I highly recommend the fettuccine found in the refrigerator section of most grocery stores. For best results, a food mill is preferred to make this; however, a food processor will work nicely as well. Served with a delicious ripe pear, a few chunks of good cheese, and a loaf of crusty bread, this soup is a complete, hearty meal."

> 3 tablespoons olive oil
> 2 large cloves garlic, minced
> 3 tablespoons dried sage
> 1 16-ounce can plum tomatoes, drained,
>   or 2 cups chopped fresh tomato
> 3 cups diced peeled red potato
> 3 cups cooked pinto or kidney beans
> 1 teaspoon salt
> Black pepper to taste
> 8 to 9 cups water
> 6 ounces fresh pasta
> Garnish: grated Parmesan cheese

1. Heat oil in a large pot over medium heat. Add garlic and sage. Cook until garlic is soft (3 to 4 minutes). Add tomatoes and cook for 4 to 5 minutes. Add 1 cup potatoes, 1 cup beans, salt, and pepper. Cook over low heat, stirring often, for 15 minutes.

2. In a separate pot, bring water to a boil. Add 2 cups boiling water to soup mixture. Simmer mixture uncovered until potatoes are tender (about 30 minutes). Transfer mixture to a food mill or a food processor. Puree.

3. Return puree to soup pot. Add remaining potatoes and 6 cups boiling water. Simmer until potatoes are almost tender (about 15 minutes). Add remaining beans and cook for 15 additional minutes. Add pasta and cook until tender (4 to 5 minutes), adding more boiling water as needed if soup becomes too thick. Adjust seasonings.

4. Ladle into serving bowls and garnish with Parmesan cheese.

Serves 8 to 10

COOK'S NOTES

SUSAN'S TORTILLA SOUP

SUSAN A. DIEHL • MARSHALL FIELD'S

"I first tried tortilla soup while I was on a ski vacation. When I got home, I tried and tried to duplicate the unique flavor of that soup, and after some persistence and creativity I finally succeeded."

> 3 pounds chicken (whole or pieces), skinned
> 2 medium onions, trimmed and halved
> 5 medium ribs celery, halved
> 18 sprigs cilantro
> 4 chicken bouillon cubes
> 10 cups water
> 12 6-inch white corn tortillas, torn into pieces
> 1 jalapeño pepper, seeded and deveined
> 2 cloves garlic, peeled

1. In a large stockpot, place chicken, onions, celery, cilantro, bouillon cubes, and water. Bring to a boil over medium-high heat. Reduce heat to medium-low and simmer uncovered for about 1 hour, until chicken can be pulled easily from the bone. Remove pot from the heat. Remove chicken and vegetables from pot. Discard vegetables. Bone and shred chicken.

2. Transfer 2 cups stock to a blender. Add tortillas, jalapeño, and garlic. Puree until smooth. Place in pot with remaining stock. Simmer over very low heat for about 30 minutes, until soup is slightly thickened. Ladle soup into individual serving bowls and serve immediately.

Serves 6 to 8

LOW-FAT BUTTERNUT SQUASH SOUP

JEANNE DeWOLFE WALTERS • HUDSON'S

"I love the creamy texture of this soup, and it's gratifying to serve friends and family a delicious dish that is tempting as well as healthful."

1 medium butternut squash (about 1½ pounds)
2 teaspoons olive oil
1 small onion, chopped
1 clove garlic, chopped

1 cup defatted chicken broth
1 cup low-fat (2%) milk
Garnish: fat-free sour cream and Hungarian sweet paprika

1. Preheat oven to 400°F.

2. Cut squash lengthwise, scoop out and discard seeds and stringy material, and bake, cut-side down, for 50 to 60 minutes. Remove from oven and let stand. When squash is cool enough, cut in half and discard seeds. Spoon pulp into a bowl and set aside.

3. In a small nonstick saucepan, heat oil over medium heat. Add onion and garlic and cook gently, stirring often, until onion begins to soften (4 to 5 minutes). Transfer onion mixture, squash, and chicken broth to a food processor or a blender. Process until smooth. Add milk and blend thoroughly.

4. Soup may be served hot or chilled. For hot soup, heat over low heat until thoroughly warmed (4 to 6 minutes). For chilled soup, cover and refrigerate until thoroughly chilled (about 45 minutes).

5. Ladle soup into individual bowls, top with a dollop of sour cream and a dash of paprika, and serve.

Serves 4

COOK'S NOTES

COOK'S NOTES

AUNTIE KAREN'S POTATO SOUP

KAREN JANE ALTMAN • DAYTON'S

"My southern mother and my equally southern grandmother used to prepare this soup in a large cast-iron kettle while corn bread baked in the oven, filling the kitchen with the aroma of simmering vegetables and freshly baked bread."

> ¼ cup butter or olive oil
> 4 ribs celery, diced fine
> 2 medium carrots, diced fine
> 1 medium onion, diced fine
> 4 cloves garlic, minced
> Salt and freshly ground black pepper to taste
> 4 medium Idaho potatoes, cut into ¾-inch cubes
> 1 10-ounce package frozen corn
> 2 cups water
> 2 cups milk
> 2 cups wide egg noodles

1. In a large pot, heat butter or oil over medium heat. Add celery, carrots, onion, garlic, salt, and pepper. Cook, stirring often, until carrots begin to soften (6 to 7 minutes). Add potatoes, corn, and water. Increase heat to medium-high and bring mixture to a boil. Reduce heat to medium-low and simmer uncovered until potatoes are almost tender (about 20 minutes).

2. Add milk and noodles. Cook over medium-low heat until noodles are tender (about 10 minutes). Adjust salt and pepper to taste and serve.

Serves 10

NONFAT CREAMED CAULIFLOWER SOUP

ED LOWENSTERN • MARSHALL FIELD'S

"This soup is virtually fat-free, has plenty of delicious, good-for-you vegetables, and, paired with a salad, is a tasty and satisfying meal."

1 cup elbow macaroni
1 medium head cauliflower (about 1½ pounds)
2 10¾-ounce cans defatted condensed chicken broth
2 10¾-ounce cans water
1 large onion, chopped
2 medium carrots, chopped
2 tablespoons chopped fresh dill or 1 tablespoon dried
Salt to taste

1. Cook macaroni in boiling water until it is very soft (about 10 minutes). Meanwhile, cut cauliflower stems into 1-inch pieces. Cut flowerets into small pieces. Set aside.

2. Drain macaroni and place in a food processor or blender. Add broth and process until smooth. Transfer to a bowl, stir in water, and set aside.

3. Boil onion, carrots, and cauliflower stems until all vegetables are very tender (15 to 18 minutes). Drain. Place in the food processor or blender and process until smooth. Pour into macaroni-broth mixture and stir.

4. Cook cauliflower flowerets in boiling water until crisp-tender (5 to 7 minutes). Drain and return to cooking pot. Add broth-vegetable mixture, dill, and salt. Simmer over low heat, stirring frequently, until thoroughly heated (4 to 5 minutes). Serve.

Serves 6 to 8

COOK'S NOTES

SCALLOP CHOWDER

CELIA MANLOVE • DAYTON'S

"My mother was a master at stretching the grocery budget to feed a family of 8, but on special occasions this was one of her favorite recipes to make. This chowder is terrific with homemade rolls and a green salad."

4 tablespoons butter
1 medium onion, sliced
1 teaspoon dried thyme
3 cups diced peeled red potato
1 cup diced celery
2 quarts hot water
2 teaspoons salt
⅛ teaspoon black pepper
2 16-ounce cans diced tomatoes, undrained
1½ cups diced carrot
2 pounds sea scallops, cut in half crosswise

1. In a large pot, melt butter over medium heat. Add onion and thyme and cook until onion begins to soften (about 5 minutes). Add potato, celery, water, salt, and pepper. Cover, increase heat to medium-high, and bring to a boil.

2. Reduce heat to medium-low and add tomatoes with their liquid and carrot. Simmer gently, uncovered, for 1 hour.

3. Add scallops and cook just until cooked through (4 to 5 minutes). Adjust seasonings to taste and serve.

Serves 12

MINNESOTA WILD RICE CHEESE SOUP

ELAINE JORGENSEN • DAYTON'S

"I have sent this recipe along with a package of 'Minnesota' wild rice to friends in San Francisco. They report that the West Coast is thoroughly enjoying a taste of the Midwest and saying 'yum-yum.'"

> ½ cup wild rice
> 1 cup water
> ¼ teaspoon salt
> ½ pound sliced bacon
> 1 medium onion, chopped
> 1 pound processed American cheese, cut into small cubes
> 2 10¾-ounce cans condensed cream of potato soup
> 1 quart half-and-half

1. Rinse rice thoroughly. Drain. Transfer to a small saucepan and add water and salt. Bring to a boil over medium-high heat. Cover, reduce heat to low, and simmer for 20 to 40 minutes (the longer the wild rice cooks, the softer it will be). Remove pan from heat and set aside.

2. In a very large deep frying pan, cook bacon over medium-high heat until crisp. Drain on paper toweling. Place onion in bacon drippings and sauté over medium heat until translucent (3 to 4 minutes). Add cheese and cook, stirring constantly, until cheese is melted. Stir in soup and half-and-half.

3. Reduce heat to low. Drain any excess water from rice. Add rice to soup mixture. Crumble bacon and add to mixture. Simmer, stirring occasionally, for 10 minutes, uncovered, until soup is thick.

Serves 8

COOK'S NOTES

JIM'S SPICY CAJUN RED BEAN SOUP

JAMES A. VITEK • DAYTON'S

"Our family loves spicy foods, and this hearty soup does an admirable job of warming the taste buds."

2 cups dried red beans
1 pound bacon, diced
1 medium onion, diced
3 cloves garlic, minced
12 to 14 cups water
1 28-ounce can crushed tomatoes
¼ cup Cajun seasoning
½ cup wild rice
½ cup brown rice
1 medium green or red bell pepper
1 cup diced celery, if desired
1 10-ounce package frozen corn

1. Place beans in a large pot. Cover with cold water and let soak overnight.

2. Drain beans and set aside. Rinse and dry pot. Place bacon in pot and cook over medium heat until it is browned but not crisp. Drain and discard fat. Add onion and garlic and cook, stirring constantly, for 1 minute. Add 3 quarts water, beans, tomatoes, and seasoning. Stir well.

3. Add rice, bell pepper, and, if desired, celery. Stir, increase heat, and bring mixture to a boil. Reduce heat to low, cover, and simmer until beans are just tender (2 to 3 hours), adding more water if necessary. Add corn and simmer for 20 minutes more. Serve.

Serves 12

COOK'S NOTES

• SOUPS AND SALADS •

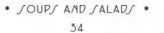

NACHO CHEESE SOUP

PAM BOE • DAYTON'S

"I like trying to duplicate restaurant dishes that my husband and I have enjoyed. This particular effort resulted in a soup that was even better than the one we'd first had."

4 tablespoons butter or margarine
6 tablespoons all-purpose flour
2 cups milk
2 cups half-and-half
2 cups chicken broth
1 pound American cheese, cubed
1 cup picante sauce
2 cups shredded cooked chicken
Tortilla chips for garnish

1. In a large saucepan, melt butter or margarine over medium heat. Add flour and cook, stirring constantly, for 1 minute. Gradually whisk in milk and half-and-half. Cook, stirring often, until mixture reaches a simmer.

2. Add chicken broth and stir. Add cheese, picante sauce, and chicken and stir. Reduce heat to low and cook, stirring often, until cheese is melted and soup is smooth.

3. Ladle soup into individual bowls. Crumble tortilla chips over top of each and serve.

Serves 8

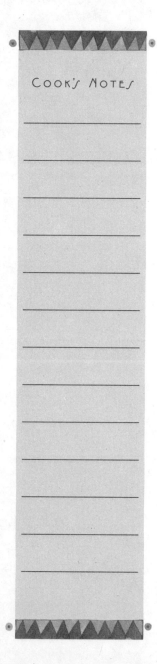

TURKEY SOUP

SANDRA HAMLIN • HUDSON'S

"My grandmother, Anna Carretta, created this soup, which started off all of our family's holiday meals when I was a child. I've served it to friends and co-workers, and they've all marveled at how truly delicious and unique it is."

Wing tips and gizzards from a large turkey
3 quarts water
2 medium carrots, peeled
1 onion, peeled
2 ribs celery
Salt to taste
2 large eggs, lightly beaten
¼ cup tomato sauce
¼ cup grated Parmesan and/or Romano cheese

1. Place wing tips and gizzards in a large pot. Cover with water and bring to a boil over medium-high heat, frequently skimming the surface with a large spoon. Reduce heat to medium-low and simmer for 1 hour. Remove and discard wing tips and gizzards.

2. Add carrots, onion, celery, and salt to broth. Simmer for 1 hour. Remove vegetables from broth. Discard onion and celery. Mash carrots and return to broth.

3. Whisking constantly, slowly add beaten eggs to broth. Cook, stirring frequently, over low heat until soup thickens (3 to 5 minutes). Do not let mixture come to a boil. Stir in tomato sauce. Stir in Parmesan cheese. Adjust salt to taste and serve.

Serves 6 to 8

CHICKEN AND SPINACH SOUP

MARY BRADLEY • HUDSON'S

"This is a traditional Middle Eastern recipe that was given to me by the mother of one of my childhood friends. Now I often make it for my own family."

> 3 to 4 pounds chicken pieces
> 10 to 12 cups cold water
> 2 10-ounce packages frozen spinach
> 2 tablespoons butter or margarine
> 2 medium onions, sliced
> 1 teaspoon ground cinnamon
> ½ teaspoon ground nutmeg
> 2 chicken bouillon cubes

1. Place chicken in a stockpot and cover with water. Cook, uncovered, over low heat for 3 hours, until meat comes away from the bone easily. Remove chicken and let cool. Strain broth into a large bowl. When chicken is cool enough to handle, remove and discard skin and bones. Chop meat into bite-sized pieces and add to broth. Cover bowl and refrigerate overnight.

2. Thaw spinach and set aside. Skim off and discard fat from top of broth. Place broth and chicken in a stockpot. In a small skillet, melt butter over medium heat. Add onion and sauté until translucent (about 4 minutes). Add onion to stockpot.

3. Place spinach in a colander and press to release excess liquid. Add spinach, cinnamon, nutmeg, and bouillon cubes to stockpot and simmer, uncovered, over low heat for 45 minutes. Serve over orzo or rice.

Serves 6 to 8

COOK'S NOTES

CHICKEN SOUP FROM HEAVEN

DIANA LUNA MARTINEZ • MARSHALL FIELD'S

"My mother has made this for years, and it's often requested by family and friends. Whether you're feeling under the weather or just wanting to savor your childhood memories, a cup of this soup makes you feel warm and cozy and reminds you of what an angel a mother really is."

1 whole chicken (about 3½ pounds)
2½ to 3 quarts water
½ teaspoon salt
1 tablespoon olive oil
1 small onion, peeled
1 clove garlic, minced

½ pound angel hair pasta, broken
  into small pieces
4 medium-sized ripe tomatoes,
  chopped
1 8-ounce can tomato sauce
¼ teaspoon black pepper

1. Place chicken in a large pot. Cover with water, add ¼ teaspoon salt, and bring to a simmer over medium heat. Reduce heat to medium-low and cook for 1 hour, until meat is tender and cooked through. Remove chicken and let cool. Refrigerate broth until fat solidifies on top. Skim off and discard fat. When chicken is cool enough to handle, remove and discard skin. Tear meat into pieces and set aside.

2. In a large skillet, heat oil over medium heat. Add onion and garlic and cook, stirring often, until onion is soft (about 5 minutes). Add dried pasta and cook, stirring often, until pasta begins to brown (4 to 5 minutes).

3. Add pasta mixture to broth. Add tomatoes, tomato sauce, chicken, remaining ¼ teaspoon salt, and pepper. Bring soup to a boil over medium-high heat and cook until pasta is tender (about 10 minutes).

Serves 8

GRANDPA'S FIREHOUSE VEGETABLE SOUP

CATHY HORVATH • MARSHALL FIELD'S

"Grandpa Mario Munarin was a Chicago fireman, and he and the other men used to take turns making dinner for the group in the firehouse kitchen. He created this recipe there."

1 pound lean ground beef
1 medium onion, diced
3 ribs celery, diced
2 cloves garlic, minced
1 26-ounce can chili beans,
  undrained
1 16-ounce can kidney beans,
  drained
1 16-ounce can diced tomatoes,
  undrained

1 8-ounce can tomato sauce
1 gallon water
½ cup lentils
½ cup pearl barley
½ cup chopped fresh parsley
Salt and black pepper to taste
3 bay leaves
2 medium Idaho potatoes, cut into
  ½-inch cubes
1½ cups small pasta shells

1. In a large pot, combine beef, onion, celery, and garlic and cook over medium heat until beef is no longer pink (8 to 10 minutes).

2. Stir in chili beans, kidney beans, tomatoes, tomato sauce, water, lentils, barley, parsley, salt, pepper, and bay leaves. Increase heat to medium-high and bring mixture to a boil. Reduce heat to medium-low and cook, uncovered, until barley is almost cooked (35 to 40 minutes).

3. Add potatoes, pasta, and, if soup is too thick, additional water. Cook until potatoes and pasta are tender (10 to 15 minutes) and serve, or cook longer for a stew-like consistency.

Serves 12 to 16

COOK'S NOTES

THICK MINESTRONE

BERNICE BAMBULIS • MARSHALL FIELD'S

"My grandparents came to this country from Italy as married teenagers. As a child I enjoyed this soup many times, but unfortunately my grandparents never wrote down the recipe. After two years of trying to duplicate that well-remembered taste, I finally re-created it."

1½ pounds lean ground beef
¼ cup olive oil
1 cup chopped onion
1 cup chopped celery
½ cup chopped green bell pepper
1 clove garlic, slivered
1 16-ounce can diced tomatoes, undrained
1 16-ounce bag frozen mixed vegetables
1 1-ounce package dry onion soup mix
1 cup diced potato
½ cup chopped fresh parsley
1 bay leaf
6 cups water
2 to 3 pounds beef soup bones, if desired
1 very small head green cabbage (about 6 ounces), chopped
Salt and black pepper to taste

1. In a large skillet, brown ground beef over medium heat. Drain and set aside.

2. In a large pot, heat oil over medium-high heat. Add onion, celery, bell pepper, and garlic and cook, stirring often, until onion is soft (6 to 7 minutes). Add ground beef and all other remaining ingredients except cabbage and salt and pepper.

3. Reduce heat to medium-low and simmer, partially covered, for 1 to 1½ hours, adding more water if soup is too thick. Add cabbage and cook for 20 minutes, until cabbage is tender. Remove and discard beef soup bones. Add salt and pepper and serve hot.

Serves 6 to 8

COOK'S NOTES

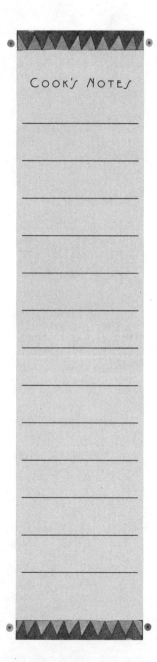
VEGETABLE MEDLEY SALAD WITH SESAME SEED DRESSING

JOAN AND TERRI TIERSKY • MARSHALL FIELD'S

"This recipe has been in our collection for many years. We always serve it at family occasions, and it's a guaranteed crowd-pleaser at block parties."

1 tablespoon butter	2 tablespoons minced onion
½ cup sesame seeds	1 clove garlic, minced
¼ cup grated Parmesan cheese	1 tablespoon sugar
1 cup sour cream or sour half-and-half	1 tablespoon tarragon-flavored white wine vinegar
½ cup mayonnaise	1 teaspoon salt
¼ cup diced green bell pepper	¼ teaspoon black pepper
¼ cup diced cucumber	2 heads lettuce (any variety)

1. In a medium skillet, melt butter over medium heat. Add sesame seeds and toast, stirring frequently, until lightly browned (about 3 minutes). Turn off heat and let seeds cool completely. Stir in cheese.

2. Make the dressing. In a medium bowl, combine sour cream, mayonnaise, bell pepper, cucumber, onion, garlic, sugar, vinegar, salt, and pepper. Mix well and refrigerate until thoroughly chilled.

3. When ready to serve, tear lettuce into bite-sized pieces and place in a large bowl. Add about three-quarters of the sesame seed mixture and about three-quarters of the dressing. Toss lightly, adding more of the dressing to taste. Sprinkle remaining sesame seed mixture over top of salad and serve.

Serves 10 to 12

FESTIVE BROCCOLI SALAD

DEB ROESER • MARSHALL FIELD'S

"I enjoy serving this salad at holiday dinners—the colors are so festive, and the flavors are a wonderful accompaniment to any entree."

> 2 bunches (about 3 pounds) broccoli
> 10 slices bacon, cooked and crumbled
> 1½ cups halved seedless red grapes
> ½ cup golden raisins
> ½ cup slivered almonds
> 1 bunch scallions, sliced
> 1 cup mayonnaise
> ½ cup sugar
> 1½ teaspoons cider vinegar

1. Trim broccoli flowerets from stems. Chop stems. Blanch flowerets and stems in boiling water until crisp-tender (4 to 6 minutes). Drain and rinse under cold water until cool. Drain well and transfer to a large bowl.

2. Add bacon, grapes, raisins, almonds, and scallions to broccoli. Toss well.

3. In a separate bowl, combine mayonnaise, sugar, and vinegar. Add to broccoli mixture and toss well.

Serves 10 to 12

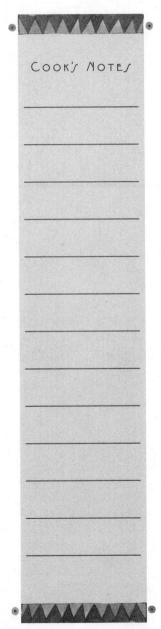

COOK'S NOTES

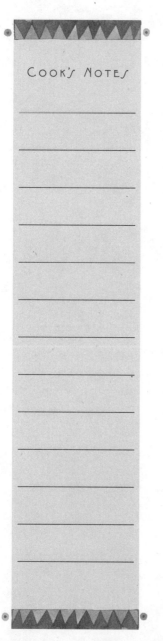

ITALIAN OLIVE SALAD

DONNA PORTELLI • DAYTON'S

This recipe is from the collection of June Patreuito and Donna Portelli. Donna writes, "Meals were always events in our childhood home, and celebrations of any kind always featured a great table of food. My mom frequently prepared this festive salad to complement whatever party menu she served."

1 6-ounce can large pitted black olives, drained
1 5¾-ounce jar pimiento-stuffed olives, drained
1 7½-ounce jar Kalamata or other Greek olives, drained
1 4½-ounce jar button mushrooms, drained
3 ribs celery, diced fine
2 tablespoons olive oil or bottled Italian salad dressing
½ teaspoon dried oregano
½ teaspoon dried basil
1 small clove garlic, pressed

1. In a mixing bowl, combine all ingredients. Cover and refrigerate for at least 6 hours or overnight. Serve chilled or at room temperature.

Serves 6 to 10

BEVERLY'S CRAZY SALAD

BEVERLY J. SHERMAN • HUDSON'S

"This is a great dish for cookouts and potluck dinners. My family loves to see this on our table at summer gatherings."

1 16-ounce can red beans, drained
1 16-ounce can garbanzo beans, drained
1 cup chopped celery
1 cup diced cucumber
½ cup diced green bell pepper
1 cup mild salsa
½ cup bottled Italian salad dressing
1 tablespoon minced cilantro
½ pound bacon
2 medium tomatoes, chopped
1 medium-sized ripe avocado, peeled, pitted, and diced

1. Combine beans, celery, cucumber, bell pepper, salsa, salad dressing, and cilantro. Cover and refrigerate for at least 3 hours or overnight.

2. In a large skillet, cook bacon over medium heat until crisp. Drain on paper toweling, let cool completely, and crumble.

3. When ready to serve, add bacon, tomato, and avocado to salad. Mix gently and serve.

Serves 6 to 8

COOK'S NOTES

PASTA PRIMAVERA

MARY PIPER • MARSHALL FIELD'S

"My sister loves this recipe. It's easy to prepare, and it is very flexible—you may add or delete vegetables according to your preference."

COOK'S NOTES

½ cup pine nuts
1 tablespoon olive oil
1½ cups broccoli flowerets
1 cup shredded carrot
1 medium red bell pepper, cut into thin strips
1 small red onion, sliced thin
1 tablespoon minced garlic
1 8-ounce jar oil-packed sun-dried tomatoes, undrained
1 4-ounce can small pitted black olives, drained
½ pound linguine
2 tablespoons chopped fresh basil
Freshly grated Parmesan cheese to taste

1. In a large dry skillet, cook pine nuts over medium heat, stirring frequently, until lightly toasted (2 to 3 minutes). Do not burn. Remove from skillet and set aside.

2. Heat oil in the skillet over medium-high heat. Add broccoli, carrot, bell pepper, onion, garlic, and tomatoes with their oil. Cook, stirring frequently, until broccoli is crisp-tender (6 to 8 minutes). Remove from heat and stir in olives.

3. Cook linguine in boiling salted water according to package directions. Drain, rinse under cold water, and drain well.

4. In a large serving bowl, place pasta, vegetable mixture, pine nuts, and basil. Mix lightly. Just before serving, sprinkle with Parmesan cheese.

Serves 2 to 4

NOTE

This salad may be served chilled or at room temperature.

COOK'S NOTES

PASTA ORIENTAL

MARGARET VAN BERGEN • DAYTON'S

"This is a lovely, delicious salad. I've served it at showers, at church functions, and at other gatherings. It's a recipe that people ask for."

6 ounces rotini
2 cups fresh snow peas, trimmed
2 cups diced cooked chicken
½ cup sliced scallion
1 8-ounce can sliced water chestnuts, drained
½ cup mayonnaise
2 tablespoons dry sherry
2 tablespoons soy sauce
1 teaspoon ground ginger
½ teaspoon black pepper
½ cup sliced toasted almonds

1. Cook pasta in boiling water according to package directions. Drain and transfer to a large bowl. Add snow peas, chicken, scallion, and water chestnuts.

2. In a separate bowl, combine mayonnaise, sherry, soy sauce, ginger, and pepper. Pour over pasta mixture and toss to combine. Chill well. Just before serving, top with toasted almonds.

Serves 6

A LITTLE BIT DIFFERENT WILD RICE SALAD

EILEEN DREW • DAYTON'S

"This dish can be prepared ahead of time, making it ideal for parties or for holiday meals. Served on a bed of purple kale and garnished with orange slices, it gets lots of oohs and aahs."

1 cup brown rice
1 cup wild rice
1 cup tiny frozen peas, thawed
1 cup chopped celery
1 cup diced red apple
1 cup chopped pitted dates
1 cup olive oil
⅔ cup red wine vinegar
½ cup orange juice
1 tablespoon honey
1 teaspoon salt

1. Cook each type of rice according to package directions. Drain well and transfer to a large bowl. Add peas, celery, apple, and dates and mix well.

2. In a separate bowl, combine oil, vinegar, orange juice, honey, and salt. Add about half of the dressing to the rice mixture and toss lightly. Add more dressing if desired and toss. Chill thoroughly before serving.

Serves 8

COOK'S NOTES

CHICKEN AND WILD RICE SALAD

LOIS F. LINDQUIST • MARSHALL FIELD'S

"This salad usually makes a command performance at our table during the holidays. I spend the summer at our home in Canada, near wild rice fields, and this is the best use of the grain I've ever come across."

1 cup wild rice
Salt or seasoned salt to taste
2 cups diced cooked chicken
1½ cups halved seedless green grapes
1½ cups pineapple chunks
1 cup sliced water chestnuts
¾ cup mayonnaise
½ cup sour cream
1 cup cashews, if desired
Lettuce leaves (any variety) for serving

1. Cook wild rice according to package directions. Salt to taste and let cool.

2. In a large bowl, mix together rice, chicken, grapes, pineapple, and water chestnuts.

3. In a separate bowl, combine mayonnaise and sour cream. Add to salad and mix lightly. Chill thoroughly.

4. Just before serving, mix in cashews, if desired. Line a serving platter with lettuce leaves, top with salad, and serve.

Serves 6

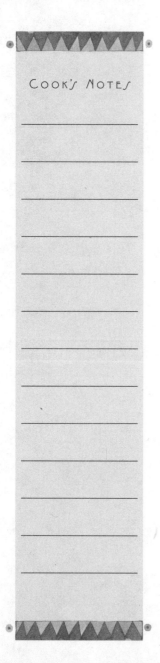

COOK'S NOTES

TABBOULEH SALAD

MARGARET M. MOURAD • HUDSON'S

"This delicious, refreshing salad is from my mother's collection. I have fond, vivid childhood memories of going out to our yard and picking the fresh mint to add to it."

1 cup coarse cracked wheat (bulgur)
2 cups cold water
5 medium tomatoes, chopped
3 medium bunches parsley, minced
1 bunch scallions, sliced
½ cup minced fresh mint leaves
Juice of 3 medium lemons
¼ cup olive oil
Salt and black pepper to taste

1. Soak cracked wheat in water for 10 minutes. Drain well and transfer to a large bowl.

2. Add tomatoes, parsley, scallions, and mint to bowl and mix well.

3. In a small bowl, mix lemon juice, oil, salt, and pepper. Pour over salad and mix well. Chill before serving.

Serves 8 to 10

COOK'S NOTES

CUCUMBER ASPIC

CHRISTOPHER HOWSE • MARSHALL FIELD'S

"I've made this dish for my mother and grandmother on Mother's Day for decades. It's now our traditional lunch for any family rite of passage or celebration."

2 large cucumbers, peeled and seeded
2 3-ounce boxes lime-flavored gelatin
2 ¼-ounce envelopes unflavored gelatin
1 teaspoon salt
2 cups boiling water
2 tablespoons white vinegar
2 teaspoons onion juice
Hot sauce to taste
1 16-ounce container sour cream (see Note)
4 small ribs celery, chopped fine
1¼ cups mayonnaise (see Note)
Juice of 4 medium limes

1. Grate cucumbers using the medium holes on a box grater. Transfer cucumber to a colander and let drain for at least 30 minutes. Press cucumber lightly to release additional liquid.

2. In a large bowl, combine gelatins and salt. Add boiling water, vinegar, onion juice, and hot sauce. Stir until gelatin dissolves. Refrigerate mixture until it begins to thicken and gel but has not set.

3. Fold sour cream, celery, cucumber, and ½ cup of the mayonnaise into mixture. Transfer mixture to a 6½- to 7-cup ring mold that has been lightly sprayed with vegetable oil spray. Refrigerate for at least 5 hours or overnight.

4. To serve, wrap bottom of mold in a hot moist towel for about 20 seconds. Place a serving plate over mold and quickly invert it. Gently remove mold from aspic. In a small bowl, combine lime juice and remaining ¾ cup mayonnaise to serve as a sauce with the aspic.

Serves 10

NOTE

For a low-fat dish, use low-fat or nonfat sour cream and low-fat or nonfat mayonnaise.

COOK'S NOTES

GRANDMA'S YUMMY SALAD

PAMELA CAVANAUGH • HUDSON'S

"My grandma, Ena Duso Blondin, made this salad for every special family occasion. When we were children, she'd take us on fall outings to collect hickory nuts for it. My daughters and I still collect hickory nuts in the fall to make grandmother's salad and to remember her."

> 1 6-ounce package lime-flavored gelatin
> 1 6-ounce package lemon-flavored gelatin
> 1 quart boiling water
> 1 quart cold water
> 2 cups heavy cream
> 1 20-ounce can crushed pineapple packed in juice, drained
> 1 cup finely chopped celery
> 2 cups (about ½ pound) shredded colby or cheddar cheese
> 1 cup coarsely chopped hickory nuts, pecans, or walnuts
> Additional whipped cream for garnish, if desired

1. In a very large bowl, combine gelatins. Add boiling water and stir for about 2 minutes, until gelatin is completely dissolved. Stir in cold water. Refrigerate for about 1 hour, until gelatin has thickened but has not set.

2. Whip cream.

3. Using a large spoon, fold pineapple into gelatin, then celery, then cheese, and finally nuts. Fold in whipped cream until thoroughly blended. Refrigerate for at least 3 hours or overnight, until set. If desired, garnish with a thin layer of whipped cream. Serve.

Serves 10 to 12

AUNT LYNN'S PRETZEL SALAD

Karen Kletter • Dayton's

"This salad, created by Lynn Ann Kletter, is almost a dessert. A Kletter family gathering isn't complete without Aunt Lynn's Pretzel Salad!"

> 2 cups (½ pound) crushed pretzel twists
> ¾ cup (1½ sticks) butter, melted
> ¾ cup plus 3 tablespoons sugar
> 1 8-ounce package cream cheese, at room temperature
> 1 8-ounce container nondairy whipped topping
> 1 6-ounce package strawberry-flavored gelatin
> 2 cups boiling water
> 1½ cups cold water
> 1 quart fresh strawberries, hulled and sliced

1. Preheat oven to 400°F.

2. In a bowl, combine crushed pretzels, melted butter, and 3 tablespoons of the sugar. Mix well and press evenly onto the bottom of a 9″ × 13″ baking pan. Bake for 8 to 10 minutes, until firm. Transfer to a cooling rack and let cool completely.

3. In a mixing bowl, combine cream cheese and remaining ¾ cup sugar. Using an electric mixer, cream at medium speed. Fold in whipped topping. Spread mixture evenly over pretzel crust.

4. In a large bowl, combine gelatin and boiling water. Stir until gelatin is completely dissolved. Add cold water. Stir in strawberries and refrigerate for about 10 minutes, until mixture just begins to thicken. Pour into pretzel crust and chill until completely set (3 to 4 hours).

Serves 24

COOK'S NOTES

BANANA SALAD

SHARALEE WILSON • HUDSON'S

"My mother, Arline Carter, invented this delicious recipe years ago. At age 83, she still makes it for all Carter family reunions in Traverse City, Michigan."

> 6 large ripe bananas
> ½ cup mayonnaise or mayonnaise-style salad dressing
> 3 tablespoons sugar
> 3 tablespoons lemon juice
> 1 cup cocktail peanuts
> 6 leaves red leaf lettuce

1. Peel bananas and cut in half lengthwise.

2. In a small bowl, combine mayonnaise, sugar, and lemon juice. Mix well.

3. Grind peanuts in a food processor or by hand, using a rolling pin.

4. Line a decorative serving bowl with lettuce leaves. Arrange 4 banana halves on lettuce. Spread about ¼ cup of mayonnaise mixture over bananas. Top with a third of the ground peanuts. Repeat process until 3-layered salad is complete. Chill before serving if desired.

Serves 8

HALIBUT IN TOMATO SAUCE

MARIA DELUCA • HUDSON'S

"This recipe belongs to my husband, Jim DeLuca. He often makes this dish for the family, and we all love it. Served with a salad, it's a light, delicious dinner."

⅓ cup olive oil
¼ teaspoon crushed red pepper
5 to 6 cloves garlic, slivered
4 medium tomatoes, chopped coarse
Salt and black pepper to taste
2 tablespoons grated Parmesan cheese
4 ½-pound halibut steaks (fresh if possible)
4 or more slices toasted garlic bread (homemade or packaged)

1. In a large frying pan, heat oil over medium heat. Add crushed pepper and garlic and sauté until garlic is light brown (about 30 seconds). Stir in tomatoes, salt, pepper, and Parmesan cheese. Arrange fish steaks in a single layer on top of tomato mixture and cook until fish is cooked through and flakes easily (about 15 minutes).

2. Transfer steaks to individual serving plates and remove any skin and bones. Top each steak with equal amounts of tomato mixture and serve with garlic bread.

Serves 4

COOK'S NOTES

LINGUINE WITH SCALLOPS, SPINACH, AND TOMATOES

THELMA MOORE • MARSHALL FIELD'S

"As part of my efforts to eat healthy foods, I created several entrees that contain no more than 2 tablespoons of oil. This is one of those recipes. We love pasta, and the fresh vegetables add extra flavor to this dish. If you'd like, you may substitute shrimp for the scallops."

1 pound linguine
2 tablespoons olive oil
3 cloves garlic, minced
4 scallions, sliced
½ cup dry white wine
6 plum tomatoes, chopped
1 4-ounce can chopped mild green chilies
Salt and freshly ground pepper to taste
½ pound bay scallops
1 10-ounce bag fresh spinach, trimmed
Garnish: grated Parmesan cheese

1. Cook linguine according to package directions.

2. While pasta is cooking, place oil in a wok or a large skillet. Heat over medium-high heat. Add garlic and scallions and cook, stirring frequently, until vegetables soften (about 1 minute). Add wine and cook for about 2 minutes, until most of the wine has evaporated. Add tomatoes, chilies, salt, and pepper and cook until tomatoes have thickened slightly (about 5 minutes).

3. Meanwhile, place scallops on top of tomato mixture. Top with spinach. Cover and cook just until spinach wilts and scallops are cooked through (about 2 minutes). Stir gently and, if necessary, adjust seasoning.

4. Transfer drained linguine to a serving platter. Top with scallop mixture, sprinkle with Parmesan cheese, and serve.

Serves 4 to 5

COOK'S NOTES

SHRIMP AND GARLIC PASTA

Susan Keldani • Hudson's

"I created this recipe after sampling a wonderful and quite similar dish at Marshall Field's Walnut Room on State Street in Chicago. It's delicious!"

> 1 pound fettuccine
> 2 tablespoons olive oil
> 1 bunch slender asparagus, trimmed
> 1 medium red bell pepper, cut into thin strips
> 2 small zucchini, sliced thin
> 1 clove garlic, chopped
> 1 8-ounce jar sliced mushrooms, drained
> Salt and freshly ground black pepper to taste
> 1 to 1½ pounds medium shrimp, peeled
> 1 bunch scallions, sliced
> Garnish: grated Parmesan cheese

1. Cook fettuccine according to package directions.

2. Meanwhile, heat oil in a wok over high heat. Cut asparagus into 1-inch pieces, add to oil, and stir-fry until asparagus begins to soften (about 3 minutes). Add bell pepper, zucchini, and garlic. Cook, stirring constantly, until vegetables are crisp-tender (2 to 3 minutes). Add mushrooms, salt, and pepper and mix well. Add shrimp. Cover and cook just until shrimp is pink (3 to 4 minutes). Stir in scallions. Adjust seasoning if necessary.

3. Transfer drained fettuccine to a serving platter. Top with shrimp mixture, sprinkle with Parmesan cheese, and serve.

Serves 6

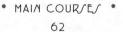

CAJUN SHRIMP AND CHICKEN PASTA

WAYNE A. HUNT • DAYTON'S

"I wanted to create a unique dish to serve at a candlelight dinner for my wife on our wedding anniversary. This is what I came up with, and it's fantastic."

3 tablespoons unsalted butter
4 skinless, boneless chicken breast halves, cut into 1-inch strips
¾ pound (about 2 cups) sliced fresh mushrooms
2 small green bell peppers, sliced thin
1 medium onion, diced

Cayenne pepper to taste
Black pepper to taste
Crushed red pepper to taste
Cajun seasoning to taste
Salt to taste
1 pound medium shrimp, peeled
1 pound fettuccine or linguine
1 15-ounce can tomato sauce

1. In a large nonstick skillet, melt 1½ tablespoons of the butter over medium-high heat. Add chicken and cook for 3 to 4 minutes, stirring often. Remove chicken from pan and set aside. Return skillet to stove.

2. Melt remaining 1½ tablespoons butter in the skillet. Add mushrooms, bell peppers, onion, and seasonings. Cook, stirring often, until onions are tender (6 to 8 minutes). Add shrimp and cook, stirring often, until shrimp is cooked (4 to 5 minutes).

3. While shrimp is cooking, cook pasta according to package directions.

4. Reduce heat to medium-low and return chicken to the skillet. Stir in tomato sauce. Adjust seasonings to taste and cook until chicken is heated.

5. Place drained pasta on a large serving platter. Top with shrimp and chicken mixture. Serve immediately.

Serves 4 to 6

COOK'S NOTES

CLAIRE'S ROSEMARY AND LEMON ROASTED CHICKEN

MILLICENT SUTHERLAND • MARSHALL FIELD'S

"My mother, Claire Sutherland, created this simple, easy-to-make recipe when, for medical reasons, she was unable to spend the effort to prepare complicated meals. It has since become one of our long-standing favorite meals."

> 1 4- to 5-pound roasting chicken
> Salt and black pepper to taste
> 1 medium lemon, sliced
> 1 small onion, sliced
> 1 sprig fresh rosemary
> 2 tablespoons all-purpose flour
> 2 tablespoons water

1. Preheat oven to 325°F.

2. Rinse chicken. Salt and pepper cavity. Stuff with lemon, onion, and rosemary. Place in a roasting pan and roast for 1¾ to 2 hours, until the juices run clear when chicken is pricked with a fork or until chicken has reached a temperature of 170°F on an instant-read thermometer. Transfer chicken to a platter and set aside. Place roasting pan on a stove burner.

3. Make the gravy. In a glass, dissolve flour in water. Add to pan drippings. Cook over medium heat, stirring constantly, until thickened.

4. Carve chicken as desired, top with gravy, and serve.

Serves 4 to 6

RASPBERRY CHICKEN

CAROLE CHANDLER • DAYTON'S

"This is a fun, elegant recipe to cook for—or with—someone special at home."

4 tablespoons butter
4 skinless, boneless chicken breast halves
Salt and white pepper to taste
⅓ cup finely chopped onion
⅓ cup raspberry vinegar
⅓ cup chicken broth
¼ cup whipping cream
1 to 1½ cups fresh raspberries

1. In a large skillet, melt butter over medium-high heat. Add chicken and cook, turning once, until browned (about 4 minutes per side). Sprinkle with salt and pepper. Remove from pan and set aside.

2. Place onion in pan and cook, stirring often, until soft (4 to 5 minutes). Increase heat to high and add vinegar. Boil until vinegar reduces by two-thirds (3 to 4 minutes). Reduce heat to medium, add broth and whipping cream, and cook until mixture thickens slightly (4 to 5 minutes). Return chicken to pan and cook, turning once, until chicken is cooked through (about 2 minutes per side).

3. Transfer chicken to a heated platter. Place raspberries in pan and reduce heat to low. Add salt and pepper to taste and cook for 1 minute. Do not stir. Pour mixture over chicken and serve immediately.

Serves 4

COOK'S NOTES

CHICKEN À LA QUEEN

Lisa Novak • Dayton's

"This is always a favorite of guests. It's very easy to make, yet it tastes as though you've been in the kitchen preparing it for hours. For an elegant luncheon, serve this dish with a fruit salad."

½ cup (1 stick) butter or margarine
½ cup all-purpose flour
1½ cups milk
1½ cups water
1 7-ounce can mushroom stems and pieces, drained
3 cups diced cooked chicken breast
1 cup frozen green peas, thawed
2 tablespoons chicken base
1 4-ounce jar sliced pimientos, drained
3 tablespoons dry white wine
1 10-ounce package frozen puff pastry shells (6 shells)

1. In a large skillet, melt butter over medium heat. Whisk in flour. Using a wooden spoon, stir constantly, slowly adding milk and water. Cook, stirring constantly, until mixture thickens.

2. Add mushrooms, chicken, peas, chicken base, pimientos, and wine. Stir thoroughly and cook for 10 minutes.

3. While chicken is cooking, prepare pastry shells according to package directions. Place prepared shells on a serving platter, fill each with equal amounts of chicken mixture, and serve.

Serves 6

COOK'S NOTES

JURGIE'S HOLLAND CHICKEN

CHRISTI CLANCY • MARSHALL FIELD'S

"My 'little' sister spent a year abroad in Holland, studying at Leiden University. When she came to visit us at Christmas, she cooked this for my family. It's a recipe that she and her 8 roommates cook quite often—it's delicious and extremely easy to prepare."

> 3 cups bite-sized pieces cooked chicken breast
> 1 large onion, minced
> 1 tablespoon olive oil
> 1 10-ounce can whole tomatoes, drained
> 1 medium green bell pepper, diced
> 1 medium red bell pepper, diced
> 1 cup sliced fresh mushrooms
> ¼ teaspoon crushed red pepper
> ½ tablespoon Ketjap (Indonesian soy sauce) or soy sauce
> ¼ pound Boursin cheese
> 4 cups cooked white or brown rice

1. In a large skillet, sauté chicken and onion in oil over medium heat until onion is soft (4 to 5 minutes). Coarsely chop tomatoes. Add bell peppers, mushrooms, tomatoes, crushed pepper, and soy sauce to skillet. Mix well. Crumble cheese over mixture. Cook until cheese is melted (about 3 minutes). Serve over rice.

Serves 4

COOK'S NOTES

CHICKEN CACCIATORE

DIANE M. JOHNSON • DAYTON'S

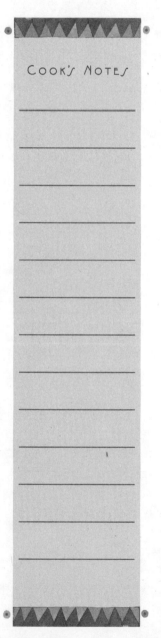

COOK'S NOTES

"When my husband and I were first married in the early sixties we, like most newlyweds, had little money. A customer of the store at which my husband worked gave him this recipe. She must have thought we would enjoy a delicious dish that wasn't too costly, and she was right. I've used the original recipe card so often it's faded."

¼ cup olive oil
1 frying chicken (about 3 pounds), cut into serving pieces
2 medium onions, sliced
2 cloves garlic, minced
1 16-ounce can diced tomatoes
1 8-ounce can tomato sauce
1 teaspoon dried basil
1 teaspoon salt
¼ teaspoon celery seed
¼ teaspoon black pepper
1 to 2 bay leaves
¼ cup dry red wine
4 to 6 cups cooked white rice or spaghetti

1. In a large skillet, heat oil over medium-high heat. Add chicken and brown well on all sides. Remove from pan and set aside.

2. Place onions and garlic in skillet. Cook, stirring frequently, until onion begins to brown (about 5 minutes). Return chicken to pan and add tomatoes, tomato sauce, and seasonings.

3. Reduce heat to low, cover, and simmer for 45 minutes. Add wine and cook, uncovered, for 20 minutes.

4. Meanwhile, cook rice or spaghetti according to package directions. Drain and keep warm.

5. Adjust chicken seasonings if necessary. Serve over rice or spaghetti.

Serves 4 to 6

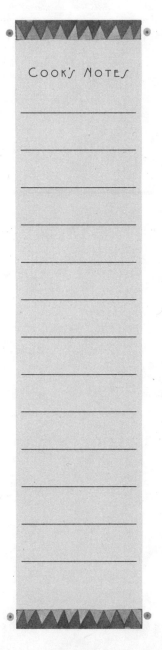

COOK'S NOTES

ITALIAN CHICKEN WITH POLENTA

GINNY GRAFITTI HODINA • MARSHALL FIELD'S

"This dish was among my mother's favorites for serving to company and at family gatherings. It reflects her northern Italian heritage, and, in addition to being delicious, it brings back wonderful memories of good times we had and of my mother's great spirit."

CHICKEN AND SAUCE

¼ cup all-purpose flour
¼ teaspoon salt
¼ teaspoon black pepper
¾ teaspoon garlic powder
1 4- to 5-pound chicken, cut into pieces
¼ cup olive oil
1 large onion, minced
1 6-ounce can tomato paste
3 cups water
½ teaspoon dried oregano
½ teaspoon dried basil
½ teaspoon dried marjoram

POLENTA

2 cups yellow cornmeal
2 teaspoons salt
1½ cups cold water
3½ cups boiling water

1. Make the chicken and sauce. In a mixing bowl, mix together flour, salt, pepper, and ¼ teaspoon garlic powder. Dredge chicken in flour mixture.

2. In a large skillet, heat oil over medium-high heat. Add chicken and brown on both sides (about 10 minutes). Remove chicken from pan and set aside.

3. Cook onion in skillet until browned (3 to 5 minutes). Add tomato paste, water, and seasonings, including remaining ½ teaspoon garlic powder, and reduce heat to low. Return chicken to pan and simmer for 1 to 1½ hours, until chicken is tender and cooked through.

4. Make the polenta. While chicken is cooking, place cornmeal in a heavy 4- to 6-quart stockpot. Add salt and cold water and, using a wooden spoon, mix well.

5. Slowly pour boiling water into cornmeal mixture, stirring constantly. Cook over medium-high heat, stirring constantly, until mixture bubbles (15 to 20 minutes). Reduce heat to low, cover, and cook for 20 to 30 minutes, stirring occasionally. Polenta should have the consistency of loose mashed potatoes.

6. Transfer polenta to a serving platter. Top with chicken and sauce and serve.

Serves 4 to 6

COOK'S NOTES

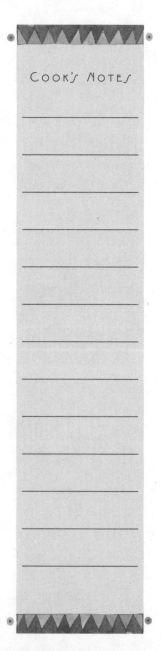
CHICKEN AND SPINACH LASAGNA ALFREDO

AMY M. GABLE • HUDSON'S

"This entree was a big success at the first dinner party I ever gave. I also served it on Mother's Day, when I wanted a special, different meal for my parents and my husband's parents."

1 pound spinach lasagna noodles
2 tablespoons olive oil
4 boneless, skinless chicken breast halves, cubed
1 teaspoon dried basil
2½ cups (1 20-ounce container) prepared Alfredo sauce (see Note)
¼ pound sliced Muenster cheese
1 cup sliced fresh mushrooms
2½ cups (about 10 ounces) shredded mozzarella cheese
¼ pound sliced Swiss cheese
¾ cup ricotta cheese
1 6-ounce jar artichoke hearts packed in oil, drained
¼ cup grated Parmesan cheese

1. Preheat oven to 350°F.

2. Prepare lasagna noodles according to package directions.

3. In a large skillet, heat oil over medium heat. Add chicken and cook until it is no longer pink (about 5 minutes). Sprinkle with basil, remove from heat, and set aside.

4. Spread ½ cup Alfredo sauce over the bottom of a 9″ × 13″ baking dish. Top with a quarter of the lasagna noodles. Spread ½ cup Alfredo sauce over noodles. Top with chicken. Place Muenster cheese over chicken.

5. Add another layer of a quarter of the lasagna noodles. Spread ½ cup Alfredo sauce over noodles. Spread mushrooms over sauce and top with 1 cup mozzarella cheese.

6. Add another layer of a quarter of the lasagna noodles. Spread ½ cup Alfredo sauce over noodles. Place Swiss cheese over sauce. Spread ricotta cheese over Swiss cheese. Top with 1 cup mozzarella cheese.

7. Add remaining noodles, Alfredo sauce, and mozzarella. Top with artichokes and sprinkle with Parmesan cheese. Bake for 35 to 40 minutes, until browned and bubbly.

Serves 6 to 8

NOTE

Prepared Alfredo sauce is available in the refrigerated section of many grocery stores.

COOK'S NOTES

CHICKEN AND BOW TIES

JAN BOHANNON • DAYTON'S

"This recipe is very special to me because it's my husband's favorite dish. He's an extremely picky eater and I never thought he would go near a sun-dried tomato, but to my surprise he loves them in this meal. I always make this for him on special occasions."

2 tablespoons olive oil
2 cloves garlic, minced
1 pound skinless, boneless chicken breasts,
    cut into 1-inch-wide strips
1 teaspoon dried basil
Salt to taste
Crushed red pepper to taste
¾ pound farfalle (bow tie) pasta
½ cup drained oil-packed sun-dried tomatoes
1½ cups chicken broth
¼ cup dry white wine
½ cup whipping cream
¼ cup grated Parmesan cheese
Garnish: additional grated Parmesan cheese

1. In a large skillet, heat oil over medium heat. Add garlic and cook, stirring often, until it begins to soften (about 3 minutes). Add chicken, basil, salt, and crushed red pepper. Cook, stirring often, until chicken is cooked (10 to 15 minutes).

2. Cook pasta according to package directions.

3. While pasta is cooking, mince the tomatoes. Add tomatoes, broth, and wine to chicken. Reduce heat to medium-low and simmer gently until mixture begins to thicken (about 5 minutes). Stir in whipping cream and cheese and simmer for 2 minutes more.

4. Place drained pasta in pan with chicken. Mix gently and transfer to a serving platter. Serve with additional Parmesan cheese at the table.

Serves 4

COOK'S NOTES

CHICKEN PAPRIKASH

Karin Marya Tansek, M.D. • Dayton's

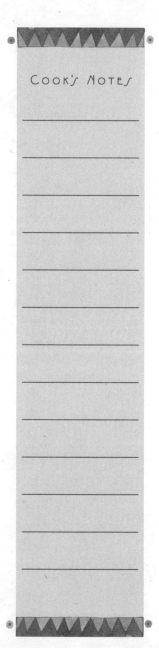

"My grandmother brought this recipe here from her native Budapest, Hungary. After I served it to a good friend, he proposed to me. We've now been happily married for 10 years."

> 3 tablespoons butter
> ½ cup chopped onion
> 1 clove garlic, minced
> 1½ tablespoons Hungarian sweet paprika
> 1½ tablespoons Hungarian hot paprika
> 1 3-pound frying chicken, cut into serving pieces
> 1 cup chicken broth
> 4 to 6 cups gnocchi (homemade or packaged fresh)
> ½ cup sour cream
> ¼ cup all-purpose flour

1. In a large skillet, melt butter over medium heat. Add onion and garlic and cook, stirring frequently, until onion is soft (about 5 minutes). Add paprika and cook, stirring frequently, for 5 minutes. Add chicken and broth. Reduce heat to low, cover, and simmer until chicken is tender and cooked through (about 40 minutes).

2. Cook gnocchi according to package directions.

3. Meanwhile, in a small bowl, combine sour cream and flour, stirring until smooth. Blend in about ½ cup of the hot liquid from the pan. Add mixture to pan and cook just until heated through. Do not boil. Serve over gnocchi.

Serves 4

CHICKEN AND ARTICHOKES

KATHIE HILTON • HUDSON'S

"This is a tasty, easy-to-make dish. It's perfect for company. Just add a Caesar salad and garlic bread, and you have a complete dinner."

> 1 tablespoon olive oil
> 1 tablespoon crushed garlic
> 4 boneless, skinless chicken breast halves, cut into bite-sized strips
> 1 pound linguine
> 1 28-ounce can diced tomatoes, undrained
> 1 14-ounce can artichoke hearts packed in water,
>   drained, rinsed, and quartered
> 1 cube chicken bouillon
> 1 tablespoon all-purpose flour
> 1 tablespoon water

1. In a large skillet, heat oil over medium heat. Add garlic and sauté for about 30 seconds, just until garlic begins to give off aroma. Add chicken and sauté until lightly browned (5 to 7 minutes).

2. Meanwhile, cook linguine according to package directions.

3. Add tomatoes and their liquid, artichokes, and bouillon to chicken. In a small glass, blend flour and water. Add to chicken. Stir well and cook for 4 to 5 minutes, until chicken is cooked through and mixture begins to boil.

4. Transfer drained linguine to a serving platter. Top with chicken mixture and serve.

Serves 4

COOK'S NOTES

SPICY CHINESE CHICKEN FETTUCCINE

MARY ANN CHENG • HUDSON'S

"The secret ingredient in this delicious dish is peanut butter, but don't tell anyone until they've tried it for themselves."

COOK'S NOTES

1 gallon water
6 bay leaves
3 pounds chicken breasts, thighs, or both
10 ounces fettuccine
6 tablespoons soy sauce
2 tablespoons sugar
1 tablespoon plus 1 teaspoon dry sherry
2 teaspoons creamy peanut butter
¼ cup vegetable oil
1 clove garlic, minced
¼ teaspoon black pepper
¼ teaspoon cayenne pepper
¼ teaspoon crushed red pepper
¼ teaspoon ground ginger
Seasoned salt to taste
¼ cup diced red bell pepper
¼ cup diced yellow bell pepper
¼ cup sliced scallion (white and green parts)
¼ cup chopped snow peas
¼ cup (1½ ounces) chopped peanuts

1. Place water and bay leaves in a large pot and bring to boil. Add chicken and return water to a boil. Cover, remove from heat, and let stand for 20 to 25 minutes. Remove chicken and let cool.

2. When chicken is cool enough to handle, remove and discard skin. Tear meat from bones, discard bones, and cut meat into 2-inch pieces.

3. Cook fettuccine according to package directions.

4. Meanwhile, make the sauce. In a bowl, combine soy sauce, sugar, sherry, and peanut butter. Stir until smooth and set aside.

5. Heat oil in a wok or a large skillet over high heat. Add garlic, black pepper, cayenne pepper, crushed red pepper, ginger, and seasoned salt to taste. Cook, stirring constantly, for 1 minute. Add chicken and toss to coat with spices. Add sauce and stir well. Add bell peppers, scallion, and snow peas. Cook just until vegetables are heated through (2 to 3 minutes).

6. Transfer drained fettuccine to a serving platter. Top with chicken-vegetable mixture. Sprinkle with peanuts and serve.

Serves 4

COOK'S NOTES

ORIENTAL CHICKEN À LA COLE

MARILYN VANDERMARK • DAYTON'S

COOK'S NOTES

"I served this dish to celebrate the one-month birthday of our grandson, Matthew Coleman Vandermark."

> 2½ tablespoons sugar
> 5 tablespoons cider vinegar
> 5 tablespoons dry vermouth
> 5 tablespoons reduced-sodium soy sauce
> 3 tablespoons lemon juice
> 4 boneless, skinless chicken breast halves
> 2 tablespoons canola oil
> 6 bamboo skewers
> 1½ cups rich chicken stock
> 4 to 6 cups cooked white rice

1. Make the marinade. In a bowl, combine sugar, vinegar, vermouth, soy sauce, and lemon juice. Mix thoroughly.

2. Cut chicken into 1-inch cubes. In a heavy-duty plastic food bag, combine chicken, ⅓ cup marinade, and 1 tablespoon oil. Seal tightly and refrigerate for at least 1 hour (up to 4 hours).

3. Soak bamboo skewers in water for 1 hour.

4. Preheat grill or broiler.

5. Set aside ½ cup marinade. Mix 1 tablespoon oil with remaining marinade. Remove chicken from bag, drain, and thread on prepared skewers. Grill or broil for 12 minutes, turning frequently and basting with marinade.

6. While chicken is cooking, make the sauce. In a small saucepan, combine chicken stock and reserved ½ cup marinade. Bring to a boil over medium heat. Boil until mixture is reduced to 1 cup (about 10 minutes). Remove from heat.

7. Place rice on a serving platter. Top with chicken and serve sauce on the side. Serve with a side dish of steamed vegetables.

Serves 4 to 6

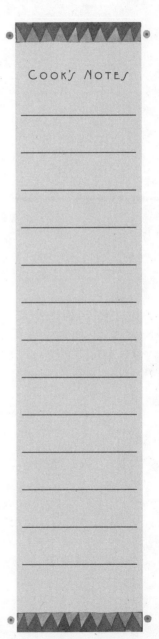

COOK'S NOTES

INCREDIBLE CORNISH HENS

GABRIELLE SAPPENFIELD • MARSHALL FIELD'S

"When I want to treat myself and my family or really impress company with a delicious dish that's low in fat, I turn to this tried-and-true recipe. It's my four-year-old's favorite dinner."

> 3 tablespoons olive oil
> 2 medium onions, chopped coarse
> 1 cup chopped fresh parsley
> 2 1½-pound Cornish hens
> Garlic salt to taste
> Lemon pepper to taste
> 4 sprigs fresh thyme or ½ tablespoon dried thyme
> About 3 cups dry white wine

1. Preheat oven to 375°F.
2. Place oil and half of the onion in a small roasting pan with a lid. In a small bowl, combine remaining onion with parsley and set aside.
3. Rinse outside and cavity of each hen. Trim and discard any excess fat. Sprinkle each cavity with garlic salt and lemon pepper. Stuff each with half of the thyme and half of the onion-parsley mixture.
4. Place hens on top of onion in roasting pan. Sprinkle with garlic salt and lemon pepper. Pour wine into the pan (wine should reach about the center of the hens' cavities). Cover and bake for 1¼ to 1½ hours, basting after about 45 minutes, until hens are cooked through and a leg tears off easily.

Serves 2

CHINESE TURKEY AND NOODLES IN SPECIAL SAUCE

JOAN H. LOWENSTEIN • HUDSON'S

"Our extended family includes a large Chinese family, so Chinese food and traditions are important to us."

1 pound fusilli or other curly noodles	*½ pound ground turkey or pork*
1 10-ounce package frozen peas and carrots	*½ cup hoisin sauce*
	½ cup tomato sauce
1 tablespoon vegetable oil	*1 teaspoon chili sauce*
1 tablespoon chopped fresh ginger	*1 large cucumber, seeded and*
1 tablespoon thinly sliced scallion	*julienned fine*
1 tablespoon chopped garlic	

1. Cook noodles according to package directions. Drain and keep warm.

2. Cook peas and carrots according to package directions. Drain and keep warm.

3. Meanwhile, place oil in a wok or large skillet and heat over medium heat. Add ginger, scallion, and garlic and stir-fry for 1 minute. Add turkey and stir-fry until it is no longer pink (2 to 3 minutes). Add hoisin, tomato sauce, and chili sauce. Reduce heat to low and cook for 5 minutes.

4. Transfer warm noodles to a large serving bowl. Place turkey mixture in a section on top of one-third of the noodles. Place cucumber in another section on top of one-third of the noodles and place peas and carrots in remaining section on top of noodles. Toss at the table.

Serves 4

COOK'S NOTES

JANE KIRKLAND'S CHRISTMAS EVE PHEASANT

LAUREL ANTHONY • DAYTON'S

"The Jack Kirkland family of Cannon Ridge Farm in Cannon Falls, Minnesota, served this every Christmas Eve, using wild game that Jack and his son David had hunted. Jane has shared this recipe with her friends and always says 'Give it to anyone who asks; just give me credit!' Everyone who is lucky enough to taste it does ask for the recipe."

⅔ cup all-purpose flour
1 teaspoon salt
½ teaspoon paprika
Black pepper to taste
3 to 4 pheasants, skinned, boned, and cut into serving pieces
6 to 8 tablespoons butter
1 pound mushrooms, sliced thick
⅔ cup dry sherry
3 10¾-ounce cans condensed cream of mushroom soup
2 cups half-and-half
½ to 1 teaspoon browning sauce, if desired

1. In a large plastic food bag, combine flour, salt, paprika, and pepper. Add pheasants, several pieces at a time, and shake to coat evenly with flour mixture.

2. In a large skillet, melt 2 tablespoons butter over medium-high heat. Add some of the pheasant pieces, being sure not to overcrowd the skillet. Brown on both sides (3 to 4 minutes per side). Remove from skillet

and set aside. Repeat process, melting more butter as needed, until all pheasant pieces have been browned.

3. Place mushrooms in the skillet and cook until slightly softened (2 to 3 minutes). Carefully pour ¼ cup of the sherry into the skillet and stir to dissolve any browned bits from the bottom of the skillet.

4. Remove skillet from heat. Add remaining sherry, soup, half-and-half, and, if desired, browning sauce and stir well. Place pheasant in a large Dutch oven. Top with soup mixture. Cover and refrigerate overnight.

5. Preheat oven to 325°F.

6. Place Dutch oven in oven and bake, covered, for 2½ hours. Uncover and cook for 30 minutes more. Serve with wild rice.

Serves 8

COOK'S NOTES

AUNT GRACE'S POT ROAST

DEL HULETT • HUDSON'S

This recipe is from the collection of Jan Erickson. Del writes, "I was served this by the family of my college sorority 'little sister' on a visit to their home. My own home was too far away to travel to during the years of World War II, and I welcomed this delicious, home-cooked meal in Detroit."

*2 tablespoons vegetable oil
1 4-pound rolled rump or cross rib roast
2 medium carrots, peeled and sliced
2 small white onions, sliced
2 bay leaves
6 whole black peppercorns
12 whole allspice berries
4 sprigs fresh parsley
1 tablespoon cider vinegar or brandy
1¼ cups boiling water
2 tablespoons dark raisins
2 teaspoons anchovy paste
1 tablespoon all-purpose flour
2 tablespoons water
Garnish: chopped dill pickle, chopped fresh parsley*

1. In a heavy Dutch oven, heat oil over medium heat. Add roast and brown on all sides (about 10 minutes). Scatter carrot and onion slices around meat. Add bay leaves, peppercorns, allspice, parsley, vinegar or brandy, and ¾ cup boiling water. Scatter raisins on top. Bring to a boil. Cover and reduce heat to low. Simmer for 2½ hours.

2. Add anchovy paste and remaining ½ cup boiling water. Cover and cook about 30 minutes more, until meat is fork-tender. Transfer roast to a serving platter and set aside for 15 minutes before slicing.

3. Remove and discard bay leaves from liquid in the Dutch oven. Strain liquid and return it to the pot. Simmer over low heat.

4. In a small bowl, whisk together flour and 2 tablespoons water. Pour into Dutch oven and cook, stirring constantly, until thickened.

5. Slice roast. Garnish with chopped dill pickle and chopped parsley and serve gravy on the side.

Serves 6 to 8

COOK'S NOTES

COOK'S NOTES

TZIMMES AND BRISKET

ELLEN LINER LASNER • DAYTON'S

"This is a very old, very traditional Jewish stew. I've modified the original recipe, using less meat and more vegetables. Every Passover and Rosh Hashanah, my family is treated to this dish, and our non-Jewish friends enjoy it as much as we do."

1 tablespoon vegetable oil
2 onions, chopped
5 cloves garlic, minced
4 pounds beef brisket
3 cups (2 12-ounce cans) beer
5 parsnips
5 carrots
3 large red potatoes
1 14½-ounce can stewed tomatoes, undrained
1 1-ounce envelope dry onion soup mix
¼ cup packed light brown sugar
¼ cup dark raisins
1 bunch fresh parsley, chopped
1 cup pitted prunes

1. Preheat oven to 450°F.

2. In a small skillet, heat oil over medium-high heat. Add onions and garlic and sauté until softened (about 3 minutes). Transfer to a large roasting pan. Place brisket fat side up on top of onion and garlic. Pour 1½ cups beer over brisket. Cover and bake for 30 minutes.

3. While brisket is baking, trim, peel, and chop vegetables. Place tomatoes and their liquid, onion soup mix, brown sugar, and raisins in a food processor. Puree.

4. Remove roasting pan from oven and reduce heat to 350°F. Scatter parsnips, carrots, and potatoes around brisket. Pour tomato puree over brisket and vegetables. Pour remaining beer over brisket and vegetables. Top with parsley. Cover pan and cook for 2½ hours.

5. Gently stir vegetables. Add prunes. Cook about 30 minutes more, until meat is fork-tender. Slice brisket and place on a serving platter. Add vegetables and prunes. Serve.

Serves 8

COOK'S NOTES

STROGANOFF

Karen Vander Wagen • Marshall Field's

"We always have this dish on Christmas Eve, when our entire family gathers around the Christmas tree before we go to church for our candlelight service."

> 1 pound beef tenderloin
> Salt and black pepper to taste
> 3 tablespoons butter
> 1 tablespoon all-purpose flour
> 1 13¾-ounce can beef broth
> 1 teaspoon dry mustard
> 1 onion, sliced thin
> 3 tablespoons sour cream

1. Cut meat into 1-inch cubes and place in a bowl. Salt and pepper to taste. Cover and set aside at room temperature for 2 hours.

2. Melt 1½ tablespoons butter in a heavy Dutch oven over medium heat. Stir in flour. Cook, stirring constantly, for 1½ to 2 minutes to form a roux. Add broth and stir until incorporated. Stir in mustard. Remove from heat.

3. In a large skillet, melt remaining 1½ tablespoons butter over medium heat. Add meat and onion. Brown meat on all sides (5 to 6 minutes). Place in the Dutch oven and stir. Stir in sour cream. Cover and cook for 20 minutes over low heat. Do not boil.

Serves 4

COOK'S NOTES

"HUPEH" SUEY

ALICE JACOBSON • MARSHALL FIELD'S

"My husband was born in China. This, a favorite childhood recipe of his, was originally prepared by the family cook."

> 1 pound round steak, sliced thin on the diagonal (see Note)
> 2 tablespoons butter
> ¾ cup soy sauce
> ½ cup water
> 1 bunch scallions (white and green parts), sliced
> 1 medium green bell pepper, cut into strips
> 3 medium ribs celery, sliced
> 6 to 8 medium carrots, grated coarse

1. In a wok or large frying pan, melt butter over medium heat. Add steak and brown on all sides (about 2 minutes). Stir in soy sauce. Stir in water. Reduce heat to low. Stir in scallions, bell pepper, celery, and carrots. Cover and cook for 10 minutes.

Serves 4 to 6

NOTE

Sliced round steak may be purchased prepackaged at most grocery stores. It is often labeled "round steak for pepper steak."

COOK'S NOTES

BEST DARN CHILI!

CATHY DUNN • HUDSON'S

"This combination of ingredients is exactly what I think chili should taste like—authentic, simple, and scrumptious. It has become my family's favorite comfort food. There's nothing like a good bowl of hot chili, especially on chilly days."

2 pounds ground sirloin
1 pound boneless pork loin, cut into very small pieces
2 tablespoons peanut oil
1 tablespoon cayenne pepper (or to taste)
1 cup chopped onion
4 cloves garlic, minced
1 tablespoon ground cumin
1 18-ounce can tomato paste
Salt to taste
¾ teaspoon paprika
1 teaspoon chili powder
1 28-ounce can tomatoes, undrained
1 15½-ounce can hot chili beans, drained
1 16-ounce can pinto beans, drained and rinsed
2 15-ounce cans black beans, drained and rinsed
¾ to 1½ cups beer
Garnish: grated cheddar cheese, minced scallion,
　　sour cream, oyster crackers

1. In a mixing bowl, combine beef and pork. Knead oil into meat.

2. Heat a large, deep-sided skillet over medium heat. Add meat and brown very well (about 10 minutes). Drain, transfer to an 8-quart stockpot,

and heat over medium heat. Mix in cayenne pepper. Stir in onion and garlic. Cook, stirring constantly, until onion becomes translucent (about 3 minutes).

3. Add cumin and tomato paste. Mix thoroughly. Stir in salt, paprika, and chili powder. Cook for 5 minutes.

4. Stir in tomatoes and their liquid and beans. Increase heat to medium-high and cook, stirring until mixture boils vigorously (4 to 5 minutes). Reduce heat to low and simmer for 10 minutes.

5. Slowly pour beer into mixture until chili reaches desired thickness. Simmer, uncovered, for 30 minutes, stirring occasionally. Ladle into individual bowls, top with cheese and scallion, and serve with sour cream and oyster crackers on the side.

Serves 12 to 14

COOK'S NOTES

MOM'S STUFFED GREEN PEPPERS

BEVERLY BERKENBILT • MARSHALL FIELD'S

"My beloved mother, who passed away two years ago, loved cooking—it was her special pleasure in life. She made the most wonderful dishes out of the simplest ingredients. I'm very happy to honor her by contributing one of her recipes."

> *2 large green bell peppers*
> *1 large onion*
> *1 large egg*
> *1 pound ground chuck*
> *1 cup fresh soft bread crumbs (about 4 slices bread)*
> *¼ cup long-grain white rice*
> *1 teaspoon salt (or to taste)*
> *¼ teaspoon black pepper (or to taste)*
> *1 10¾-ounce condensed tomato soup*
> *⅔ cup water*

1. Cut bell peppers in half lengthwise, leaving stems on. Seed, core, and devein bell peppers. Peel onion and grate in a food processor.

2. In a mixing bowl, beat egg with a fork. Add meat and knead in. Add onion, bread crumbs, rice, salt, and pepper and mix thoroughly. Form mixture into 4 equal-sized balls. Stuff a ball into each bell pepper half. Place stuffed peppers into a 4-quart pot. Pour tomato soup over peppers. Add ½ can (⅔ cup) water. Do not stir.

3. Cook over medium heat just until water begins to steam (about 3 to 4 minutes). Reduce heat to low, cover, and simmer for 20 minutes. Stir sauce gently, spoon over peppers, cover, and cook for 45 minutes more.

Serves 4

BEEF AND POTATO CASSEROLE

DORIS V. WICKS • DAYTON'S

"This recipe has been a favorite of my family's for 20 years."

2 pounds (about 5 large) Idaho potatoes,
   peeled and boiled fork-tender
1 cup heavy cream, scalded
½ teaspoon black pepper
1¼ teaspoons salt
1 pound lean ground beef
2 large onions, chopped fine
¾ cup beef broth
2 teaspoons chopped fresh parsley
½ teaspoon bouquet garni

1. Preheat oven to 400°F.

2. In a large bowl, mash potatoes. Mix in cream, ¼ teaspoon of the pepper, and ½ teaspoon of the salt. Set aside.

3. Place ground beef and onions in a large skillet over medium heat. Cook until meat is browned and onions are soft (5 to 8 minutes). Stir in broth, parsley, bouquet garni, and remaining salt and pepper. Transfer mixture to a 1½-quart baking dish and top with mashed potatoes.

4. Bake for 25 to 30 minutes, until potatoes are lightly browned.

Serves 4 to 6

COOK'S NOTES

ITALIAN MEAT LOAF

JOAN BUSSEN • DAYTON'S

"This recipe is a favorite of my family. It's easy to prepare, and it may be made ahead of time and frozen for use on busy days when cooking is a chore."

> 1 pound ground chuck
> ½ pound mild bulk Italian sausage
> ½ cup corn bread stuffing
> ¾ cup condensed chicken mushroom soup
> ⅓ cup (about 1½ ounces) shredded provolone cheese
> 1 large egg
> ½ cup dry onion soup mix (½ to ¾ envelope)
> ¼ cup chopped green bell pepper
> Salt and black pepper to taste
> 2 tablespoons ketchup

1. Preheat oven to 350°F.

2. In a large mixing bowl, combine all ingredients except ketchup. Mix thoroughly.

3. Transfer meat mixture to a 9″ × 5″ × 3″ loaf pan that has been lightly sprayed with vegetable oil spray. Drizzle ketchup on top of meat. Bake for 45 minutes, until meat loaf is crusty on top.

Serves 6 to 8

COOK'S NOTES

AUSTRIAN GOULASH

MARLENE TEMPLE • DAYTON'S

"A very dear Austrian friend gave me this recipe. I've adapted it to our measurements and available American ingredients."

1 tablespoon vegetable shortening
1 medium onion, chopped
2 cloves garlic, minced
2 pounds pork tenderloin
2 pounds cold-packed sauerkraut
2 tablespoons Hungarian sweet paprika
1 tablespoon Hungarian hot paprika
1 bay leaf
1 teaspoon dried marjoram
Caraway seeds to taste
Salt and black pepper to taste

1. Melt shortening in a Dutch oven over medium heat. Add onion and garlic. Cook, stirring frequently, until onion is tender (5 to 6 minutes). While onion and garlic are cooking, cut pork into 1-inch cubes.

2. Increase heat to high. Add pork to pot and cook, stirring often, until well browned (about 8 minutes).

3. Add sauerkraut and seasonings. Cover and simmer for 1½ to 2 hours, until meat is tender, stirring occasionally and adding water if mixture becomes too dry. Adjust seasonings if necessary. Remove bay leaf before serving.

Serves 6

COOK'S NOTES

GRILLED PORK TENDERLOIN

LAURIE KING • MARSHALL FIELD'S

"Our first child, Anna Marie, was conceived in Key West when we were visiting my sister-in-law. She made this dish during our stay, and it's been special to me ever since."

2 tablespoons soy sauce
2 tablespoons hoisin sauce
2 tablespoons dry sherry
1 tablespoon peanut oil
1½ tablespoons honey
1 tablespoon light brown sugar
½ teaspoon garlic salt
½ teaspoon ground cinnamon
2 1-pound pork tenderloins

1. In a bowl, combine all ingredients except pork. Mix well. Transfer to a large plastic food bag. Add pork. Tightly seal bag, expelling excess air. Refrigerate for at least 8 hours (up to 48 hours; the longer, the better).

2. Preheat broiler or prepare grill.

3. Grill or broil 6 to 8 inches from the heat source for 25 to 30 minutes, turning every 5 minutes, until crusty brown all over.

Serves 4 to 6

CRANBERRY PORK CHOPS

JANE M. WORKMAN • HUDSON'S

"This tasty recipe was given to me by my daughter, Mary Kruse."

1½ tablespoons butter
1½ tablespoons vegetable oil
6 6- to 8-ounce center-cut pork chops
1 cup fresh cranberries
Salt and black pepper to taste
¼ cup packed light brown sugar
1 tablespoon all-purpose flour
½ cup water
Garnish: 1 navel orange, sliced

1. Heat butter and oil in a large skillet over medium heat. Add pork chops and brown on both sides (3 to 4 minutes per side). Drain off excess fat. Add cranberries, salt and pepper, and brown sugar. Cover, reduce heat to low, and simmer for 1 hour.

2. Transfer pork chops to a warm platter. In a small glass, blend flour and water until smooth. Pour into skillet and cook, stirring constantly, until thickened (2 to 3 minutes). Pour sauce over pork chops. Garnish with orange slices.

Serves 6

COOK'S NOTES

PHYLLIS'S PORK CHOPS

PHYLLIS O. SUTCLIFFE • DAYTON'S

"This was my mother's family recipe—she often prepared it for our birthdays. It's now one of my husband's favorite dinners."

> 2 tablespoons vegetable oil
> 6 ½-pound center-cut pork chops
> Salt and black pepper to taste
> 1 tablespoon Dijon-style mustard
> 1 large onion, sliced
> 1 10¾-ounce can condensed chicken gumbo soup

1. Preheat oven to 325°F.

2. In a large skillet, heat oil over medium heat. Add pork chops and brown on both sides (3 to 4 minutes per side). Transfer to a baking dish and arrange in a single layer. Salt and pepper to taste.

3. Spread ½ teaspoon mustard over each pork chop. Top each with a slice of onion. Pour soup over pork chops. Cover baking dish with aluminum foil and bake for about 2 hours, until pork chops are fork-tender.

Serves 6

COOK'S NOTES

OVERNIGHT SENSATION

LESLIE ALEXOPOULOS • HUDSON'S

"This recipe has been a Christmas morning tradition in my family for many generations."

4 cups (about 8 slices) French or Italian bread in ½- to 1-inch cubes
1 pound sliced bacon, cooked and drained
¾ pound ham, cooked and cubed
1½ pounds bulk sausage, cooked and drained
1½ cups (about 6 ounces) shredded medium-sharp cheddar cheese
6 large eggs
1½ cups milk
½ teaspoon dry mustard
Salt and black pepper to taste
1 small onion, diced
1 small green bell pepper, diced

1. Place bread cubes in a 9″ × 13″ baking dish that has been lightly sprayed with vegetable oil spray. Top with bacon. Top bacon with ham. Crumble sausage over ham. Sprinkle cheese over sausage.

2. In a mixing bowl, lightly beat eggs. Add milk, mustard, salt and pepper, onion, and bell pepper. Whisk to combine. Pour mixture over casserole. Cover with plastic wrap and refrigerate overnight.

3. Preheat oven to 350°F.

4. Remove plastic wrap from casserole. Bake casserole for 1 hour, until firm and lightly browned.

Serves 8

COOK'S NOTES

ROCK and ROLL PIZZA

LINDA SWANSON • MARSHALL FIELD'S

"This recipe was created by my 10-year-old nephew, Brett Sitter. Brett tried 4 or 5 times before he was satisfied that the recipe was perfect. He's a very determined young man—especially when he thinks the result will be pizza for dinner more often. This is great."

¾ pound mild bulk pork sausage
1 10-ounce can prepared refrigerated pizza crust
1 8-ounce can tomato sauce
½ tablespoon Italian seasoning
¼ cup sliced black olives
¼ cup chopped onion
¼ cup chopped green bell pepper
¼ cup chopped red bell pepper
1 8-ounce can crushed pineapple packed in juice, well drained
1½ cups (about 6 ounces) shredded mozzarella cheese

1. Preheat oven to 425°F.

2. In a skillet over medium heat, brown sausage (6 to 7 minutes). Drain off excess fat and set aside.

3. Unroll pizza crust and place on a floured work surface. Stretch to 9″ × 13½″. Spread tomato sauce evenly over crust. Sprinkle Italian seasoning over sauce. Layer with sausage, olives, onion, and bell pepper.

4. In a colander, gently press excess liquid from pineapple. Spread pineapple evenly over other pizza ingredients. Top with 1 cup of the cheese.

5. Starting with a long side, roll up jelly-roll style. Pinch seams to seal. Using a serrated knife, cut into 9 1½-inch slices. Using a spatula, transfer slices to a 9-inch square baking pan that has been lightly sprayed with vegetable oil spray.

6. Bake for 30 minutes, until pizza crust is light golden brown. Remove from oven and let cool for 3 minutes. Sprinkle with remaining ½ cup cheese. Serve immediately.

Serves 6 to 8

COOK'S NOTES

SAUSAGE MANICOTTI

BRIDGET HAUBOLD • HUDSON'S

"After my husband and I moved from Wisconsin to Michigan, I called my mom, Maureen Hilbert, and told her how homesick I was. She sent me this recipe, and preparing it brought back fond memories of Mom and Dad."

1 pound mild bulk pork
    sausage
2 15-ounce cans tomato sauce
1 6-ounce can tomato paste
¼ cup water
½ tablespoon light brown sugar
2 cups ricotta cheese

3 cups (about ¾ pound) shredded
    mozzarella cheese
1 medium egg, beaten
1 teaspoon chopped fresh parsley
12 manicotti noodles, cooked and
    drained
Garnish: grated Parmesan cheese

1. Preheat oven to 350°F.

2. In a large skillet, brown sausage over medium heat (about 10 minutes). Drain off excess fat. Transfer half of the sausage to a medium bowl and set aside. Return skillet to burner and reduce heat to low. Place tomato sauce, tomato paste, water, and brown sugar in skillet with remaining sausage. Stir well and simmer for 15 minutes.

3. While sauce is simmering, add ricotta, 2 cups mozzarella cheese, egg, and parsley to sausage in bowl. Mix well.

4. Pour a third of the sauce into a 9″ × 13″ baking dish. Gently stuff each noodle with cheese mixture and place in dish. Pour remaining sauce over noodles. Top with remaining mozzarella. Bake, uncovered, for 20 minutes. Sprinkle with grated Parmesan cheese and serve.

Serves 6

BLACK BEAN LASAGNA

JOYCE MUNDAHL • DAYTON'S

"I once served my family a lasagna that I had purchased ready-made instead of my own from-scratch dish. They were horrified, and asked that I never do that again. This recipe is definitely a family favorite."

12 lasagna noodles, cooked according to package directions
2 10-ounce cans diced tomatoes with chilies, undrained
1 6-ounce can tomato paste
1 16-ounce can black beans, rinsed and drained
½ teaspoon ground cumin
½ teaspoon chili powder (or more to taste)
1½ pounds ricotta cheese
2 large egg whites
2 cups (about ½ pound) shredded mozzarella cheese

1. Preheat oven to 350°F.

2. Cook noodles according to package directions. Drain.

3. While noodles are cooking, combine tomatoes and tomato paste in a medium bowl. In a separate bowl, combine beans and seasonings. In a third bowl, combine ricotta cheese and egg whites.

4. Place half of the noodles in a 9″ × 13″ baking pan. Spread half of the tomato mixture over noodles. Top with half of the ricotta cheese mixture. Top with half of the beans. Sprinkle 1 cup mozzarella cheese over beans. Repeat process. Bake for 35 to 45 minutes, until heated through.

Serves 6 to 8

COOK'S NOTES

ASPARAGUS ENCHILADAS

PATRICIA CHIPMAN • HUDSON'S

"We have a summer home in asparagus territory on Lake Michigan and are always looking for new ways to use this wonderful vegetable. This recipe is a big hit around here."

½ cup (1 stick) butter
3 cups (about ½ pound) chopped fresh mushrooms
1 large onion, diced
½ cup diced green bell pepper
1 4-ounce can diced green chilies, drained
¼ cup all-purpose flour
3 cups chicken broth
1 cup sour cream
1½ cups (about 6 ounces) shredded Monterey Jack cheese
36 medium asparagus spears, blanched
12 6-inch flour tortillas
¼ cup chopped cilantro

1. Preheat oven to 450°F.

2. In a large skillet, melt 4 tablespoons butter over medium heat. Add mushrooms, onion, bell pepper, and chilies and sauté until onion is tender (about 5 minutes). Remove vegetables from skillet and set aside.

3. Return skillet to burner, add remaining 4 tablespoons butter, and melt over medium heat. Stir in flour, blending well. Add broth and stir until thickened (about 10 minutes). Blend in sour cream and ½ cup of the cheese. Remove skillet from heat.

4. Place 3 asparagus spears in the center of each tortilla. Top each with ¼ cup vegetable mixture and 2 tablespoons sour cream sauce. Roll up tortillas and place in a single layer in a 9″ × 13″ baking dish. Pour remaining sauce over tortillas. Sprinkle with remaining cheese.

5. Bake for 45 minutes. Remove from oven, sprinkle with cilantro, and serve.

Serves 6 to 8

COOK'S NOTES

PASTA CON PEPE

LIA LOCHIRCO • HUDSON'S

"This recipe is special to me because I received it from my best friend, Grace, who now lives in Italy."

2 tablespoons olive oil
1 small onion, chopped
1 medium red bell pepper, diced fine
1 medium yellow bell pepper, diced fine
1 medium green bell pepper, diced fine
1 28-ounce can whole tomatoes, pureed
1 tablespoon sugar
Salt to taste
½ teaspoon black pepper
1 cup whipping cream
1 pound fettuccine
Garnish: grated Parmesan cheese

1. Heat oil in a large skillet over medium heat. Add onion and bell peppers. Cook, stirring frequently, until peppers begin to soften (4 to 5 minutes). Add tomato puree, sugar, salt, and pepper. Reduce heat to low and simmer until slightly thickened (about 25 minutes). Stir in cream. Adjust seasonings, if necessary, and heat through.

2. While sauce is simmering, cook fettuccine according to package directions.

3. Transfer fettuccine to a serving bowl. Top with sauce. Sprinkle with Parmesan cheese and serve.

Serves 4

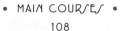

SHELLIE'S PERFECT PASTA

SHELLIE HERMAN • HUDSON'S

*"My young son acquired a love for what he calls 'noodles' at a very early age.
I created this and other simple pasta dishes to satisfy his 'noodle' cravings."*

1 pound angel hair pasta
⅓ cup olive oil
1 tablespoon chopped garlic
6 plum tomatoes, chopped
¼ cup chopped fresh basil
1½ cups (about 6 ounces) grated Asiago cheese

1. Cook pasta according to package directions. Drain and keep warm.

2. While pasta is cooking, heat oil in a medium skillet over medium heat. Add garlic and sauté until softened (about 3 minutes). Add tomatoes, reduce heat to low, and simmer for 4 minutes. Add basil and simmer for 1 minute more.

3. Transfer pasta to a serving bowl. Top with sauce. Add cheese and toss well.

Serves 4 to 6

COOK'S NOTES

POTATO ZUCCHINI PIE

Suzanne Bosserd • Hudson's

"Everyone loves seeing this meatless entree on the dinner table at my family's annual cousin get-together."

> 2 pounds (6 to 7 medium) red potatoes
> 1 pound (about 2 medium) zucchini, grated
> 2 large eggs
> ¼ teaspoon salt
> ½ pound mozzarella cheese, shredded (about 2 cups)
> ½ cup grated Parmesan cheese
> ¼ cup minced onion
> ½ teaspoon Italian seasoning
> 2 tablespoons cornflake crumbs
> 2 tablespoons butter or margarine, cut into small pieces

1. Bring a large pot of water to a boil. Add potatoes and boil for 25 minutes (potatoes will be a bit hard). Drain, let cool, and grate.

2. Preheat oven to 400°F.

3. In a large bowl, beat eggs. Mix in potatoes and zucchini. Add salt, mozzarella, Parmesan, onion, and Italian seasoning. Mix thoroughly.

4. Pour mixture into a 10-inch pie dish that has been lightly coated with vegetable oil spray. Sprinkle with cornflake crumbs and dot with butter or margarine.

5. Bake for 30 to 35 minutes, until lightly browned.

Serves 6

•SIDE DISHES•

ASPARAGUS SESAME MIX

AYAKO OLSSON • DAYTON'S

"My grandson did not like asparagus (he calls it 'aspara-grass') until he tried this dish. It definitely met with his approval."

Salt to taste
1 bunch slender asparagus (about 1 pound),
    cut into 1½-inch lengths
3 tablespoons sesame seeds
¼ cup soy sauce
1 tablespoon rice wine or white wine

1. Fill a large pot three-quarters full of water. Add salt and bring to a boil. Place asparagus in water and boil until crisp-tender (4 to 6 minutes). Do not overcook. Drain. Immediately hold asparagus under cold water until cool. Place in a large bowl and set aside.

2. Make the dressing. Place sesame seeds in a small dry skillet. Cook over medium-high heat until seeds begin to take on a pale gold color (about 2 minutes). Do not burn. Crush seeds in a spice grinder or with a mortar and pestle until seeds are flaky. In a small bowl, combine seeds, soy sauce, and wine.

3. Pour dressing over asparagus and toss well. Place equal amounts on individual serving dishes.

Serves 4

COOK'S NOTES

CORN-BROCCOLI CASSEROLE

JENIFER MURRAY • HUDSON'S

"This is a family tradition at Thanksgiving and Christmas. It's perfect with turkey, dressing, and all the other trimmings—and it's very easy to make."

½ box (about ¼ pound) chicken-flavored crackers
½ cup water
1 10-ounce package frozen chopped broccoli
½ cup (1 stick) butter at room temperature
1 14¾-ounce can cream-style corn
1 15¼-ounce can whole corn kernels, drained

1. Preheat oven to 350°F.
2. Place crackers in a plastic food bag. Expel air from bag, seal tightly, and, using a rolling pin, crush crackers. Set aside.
3. Place water in a medium saucepan. Bring to a boil over high heat. Add broccoli, cover, and cook for 3 minutes. Drain.
4. Return saucepan to stove. Place butter in pan and melt over low heat. Remove pan from heat. Stir in broccoli. Add crushed crackers and corn. Mix well.
5. Place mixture in a 2-quart casserole dish. Bake for 35 to 40 minutes, until lightly browned on top.

Serves 10

CAULIFLOWER SUPREME

KAYE CAMPBELL • DAYTON'S

"This wonderful vegetable dish has been a part of our family's holiday meals for 30 years."

1 large head cauliflower (2 to 2½ pounds), broken into flowerets
⅓ cup butter
1 8-ounce jar sliced mushrooms, drained
¼ cup diced green bell pepper
¼ cup all-purpose flour
2 cups milk
1 teaspoon salt
1 cup (about 4 ounces) shredded cheddar cheese

1. Preheat oven to 375°F.

2. Bring a medium pot of water to a boil. Add cauliflower and boil until tender (8 to 10 minutes). Drain well and set aside.

3. Make the sauce. In a medium saucepan, melt butter over medium-high heat. Add mushrooms and bell pepper. Stir in flour and cook, stirring constantly, for 1 minute. Add milk and salt. Cook, stirring frequently, until mixture thickens (3 to 4 minutes).

4. Place half of the cauliflower in a greased 2½-quart casserole dish. Top with half of the sauce. Sprinkle ½ cup cheese over sauce. Repeat process. Cover and bake for 15 to 20 minutes, until heated through.

Serves 6 to 8

COOK'S NOTES

SPINACH À LA ARTICHOKE

ALYCE CUELLER • MARSHALL FIELD'S

"Grandma always served this wonderful vegetable dish with her delicious pork roast for a Christmas Eve meal."

> 2 10-ounce packages frozen chopped spinach, thawed
> 2 6-ounce jars marinated artichoke hearts, drained
> Salt and black pepper to taste
> 1 8-ounce package cream cheese, at room temperature
> 6 tablespoons milk
> 2 tablespoons mayonnaise
> ⅓ cup Parmesan cheese

1. Preheat oven to 350°F.

2. In a colander, drain spinach, squeezing as much excess water from it as possible. Transfer spinach to a 2-quart casserole dish. Add artichokes and salt and pepper.

3. In a mixing bowl, combine cream cheese, milk, and mayonnaise. Pour over spinach mixture. Mix together gently and sprinkle with cheese.

4. Bake, uncovered, until top is lightly browned (35 to 40 minutes). Serve hot.

Serves 6

ARNIE'S HOMINY

LINDA NEWSOME • HUDSON'S

"This is my son Arnie's favorite side dish, especially when it's served with pinto beans and corn bread."

2 strips bacon, cut into small pieces
1 medium onion, chopped
1 14½-ounce can white hominy
1 8-ounce can tomato sauce
Dash hot sauce, if desired

1. Cook bacon in a large, deep skillet over medium heat until crisp. Drain bacon on paper toweling.

2. Place onion in bacon drippings and sauté over medium heat until onion is translucent (about 3 minutes). Add hominy, tomato sauce, and bacon. Simmer over low heat for 5 minutes, stirring occasionally. Add hot sauce, if desired, and serve.

Serves 4

COOK'S NOTES

BARBECUED LIMA BEANS

ARLENE CHISHOLM • MARSHALL FIELD'S

"This dish is the perfect accompaniment to the smoked brisket we like to prepare for family and friends."

> *1 pound dried lima beans*
> *2 quarts cold water*
> *1 10¾-ounce can condensed tomato soup*
> *1 cup packed dark brown sugar*
> *1 teaspoon dry mustard*
> *1 large onion, chopped*
> *1 medium green bell pepper, chopped*
> *1 tablespoon Worcestershire sauce*
> *¼ cup ketchup*
> *½ pound slab bacon, cut into ½-inch cubes and cooked through*
> *½ pound salt pork, cut into ½-inch cubes and cooked through*

1. In a large pot, cover lima beans with water. Soak overnight.

2. Preheat oven to 350°F.

3. Place pot on stove. Cook uncovered over medium heat for about 1 hour, until beans are tender. Drain.

4. Place soup in a large bowl. Add brown sugar and stir until dissolved. Stir in mustard, onion, bell pepper, Worcestershire sauce, and ketchup. Add bacon, salt pork, and beans and mix well.

5. Pour mixture into a 9″ × 13″ baking dish. Bake for 1 hour, until bubbly and browned on top.

Serves 8 to 10

GRAMPA'S BAKED BEANS

MAUREEN CALIMAN • HUDSON'S

"My grandfather, Dorn Comstock, loved to cook. This is my favorite of his recipes. When I moved away to start my own family, my grandmother, Genevera, asked Grampa to write it down for me. The aroma of this baking always brings back many fond memories."

> 4 cups dried navy beans, soaked overnight
> ½ pound bacon, cut into 1- to 2-inch pieces
> 1 sweet onion, diced fine
> ⅓ cup packed dark brown sugar
> ⅓ cup honey
> 2 teaspoons salt or to taste
> 1 teaspoon black pepper
> 1 teaspoon dry mustard
> Water

1. Preheat oven to 275°F.

2. Drain beans, reserving soaking liquid. Transfer beans to a 3-quart casserole dish. Add bacon, onion, brown sugar, honey, salt, pepper, and mustard. Add enough soaking liquid to cover beans. (If more liquid is necessary, add water.)

3. Bake uncovered for 2 hours. Cover tightly and bake until beans are tender (2 to 3 hours), adding water as necessary so beans don't dry out.

Serves 10 to 12

COOK'S NOTES

DAUPHIN POTATOES

SALLY JOHNSON • DAYTON'S

"This is one of the most elegant ways to serve potatoes that I know. It's wonderful with roast duck."

COOK'S NOTES

4 large russet potatoes
6 to 8 cloves garlic, minced
2 cups (about ½ pound) shredded Gruyère cheese
Salt and white pepper to taste
1½ cups whipping cream

1. Peel potatoes. Cut into ⅛-inch-thick slices. Soak in ice water for several hours or overnight. Drain well and pat dry.

2. Preheat oven to 400°F.

3. Place one quarter of the potatoes in a single layer in a 9″ × 13″ or a 7″ × 12″ baking dish. Sprinkle with a quarter of the garlic and a quarter of the cheese. Salt and pepper to taste. Repeat process 3 times. Pour cream evenly over top.

4. Cover and bake for 30 minutes. Remove cover and continue to bake until potatoes are tender and top is nicely browned (about 30 minutes more). Remove from oven and let stand for 10 to 15 minutes. Serve.

Serves 4 to 6

GOURMET POTATOES

DEBRA J. EDWARDS • MARSHALL FIELD'S

"I prepare this dish every Christmas Eve and serve it with a baked ham. It's easy to make ahead of time, and it's very popular with our family—there are never leftovers."

6 medium Idaho potatoes, boiled until almost tender,
    peeled, and chilled
2 cups (about ½ pound) shredded cheddar cheese
1½ cups sour cream
½ cup chopped onion
1 teaspoon salt
½ teaspoon black pepper
4 tablespoons butter, cut into pieces,
    plus butter for casserole dish

1. Preheat oven to 350°F.
2. Using a coarse grater, shred potatoes. Place in a large bowl. Add all other ingredients except butter. Mix thoroughly.
3. Transfer mixture to a buttered, 2-quart casserole dish. Dot with butter pieces. Bake until golden brown on top (about 30 minutes).

Serves 6

COOK'S NOTES

HOT POTATO SALAD

JOAN HODSDON • HUDSON'S

"When I was dating my future husband in the early 1950s, I was given this recipe by his mother. She was everything I could ever want in a grandmother to my children, and I think of her every time I serve this dish."

6 to 8 large red potatoes, boiled, peeled, and cubed
1 small rib celery, sliced
1 small onion, chopped fine
Salt and black pepper to taste
1 pound sliced bacon
⅔ cup sugar
2 tablespoons all-purpose flour
⅓ cup cider vinegar
4 large hard-cooked eggs, sliced
Garnish: paprika, if desired

1. In a large serving bowl, combine potatoes, celery, onion, salt and pepper. Mix thoroughly and set aside.

2. In a large skillet, cook bacon over medium heat until crisp. Drain on paper toweling. Add sugar, flour, and vinegar to bacon drippings in skillet and stir to combine. Cook over medium heat, stirring constantly, for 3 to 4 minutes, until sauce is clear and thick.

3. Pour sauce over potato mixture and toss to coat. Crumble bacon and add to mixture, tossing well. Arrange egg slices on top, sprinkle with paprika, if desired, and serve.

Serves 6 to 8

SWEET POTATO DELIGHT

RUTH VANDEN BOSCH • HUDSON'S

"We enjoy this dish on Thanksgiving, Christmas, and Easter. Maybe that's why we associate it with good times and good meals."

3 cups mashed cooked sweet potato
½ cup granulated sugar
2 large eggs, lightly beaten
½ cup orange juice
½ cup butter, softened, plus butter for casserole dish
1 cup packed light brown sugar
1 cup finely chopped pecans
⅓ cup all-purpose flour

1. Preheat oven to 350°F.

2. In a food processor or a large bowl, combine potato, granulated sugar, eggs, orange juice, and ¼ cup of the butter. Process until smooth and transfer to a lightly buttered 2-quart casserole.

3. In a small bowl, combine remaining ¼ cup butter, brown sugar, pecans, and flour. Blend until mixture is crumbly and well blended. Sprinkle over potatoes.

4. Bake for 35 minutes, until heated through.

Serves 8

COOK'S NOTES

JO'S APPLE SUPREME

JOSEPHINE PENNUCCI • HUDSON'S

"This is a very old recipe, passed down from my mother's family to me."

3 Granny Smith or other tart apples, peeled, cored, and sliced
4 tablespoons butter
½ cup packed dark brown sugar
1 teaspoon lemon juice
1 40-ounce can sweet potatoes, drained
1 teaspoon ground cinnamon
¼ teaspoon ground nutmeg
½ cup chopped walnuts

1. Place apples, butter, and brown sugar in a large skillet. Cook over medium heat for 7 to 8 minutes, stirring occasionally, until apples are fork-tender.

2. Add lemon juice and sweet potatoes. Mix well. Stir in cinnamon and nutmeg. Reduce heat to low and cook for 15 to 20 minutes, until bubbly and thick. Transfer to a serving bowl and top with walnuts.

Serves 6 to 8

BEST-EVER CURRY RICE

COLLEEN M. CHMELKO • HUDSON'S

"This is always a favorite at potluck gatherings. It's easy to prepare, and it goes well with many meat, fowl, and fish dishes."

> 2 cups long-grain white rice
> 1 cup vegetable oil
> ½ cup soy sauce
> 2 to 4 tablespoons curry powder
> 1 tablespoon sugar
> 1 teaspoon celery salt
> ½ teaspoon garlic powder
> 1 cup frozen tiny peas
> 1 cup diced celery
> ½ cup chopped scallion
> 1 4¼-ounce can shrimp, rinsed and drained
> Salt and black pepper to taste

1. Cook rice according to package directions.

2. While rice is cooking, mix together oil, soy sauce, curry powder, sugar, celery salt, and garlic powder in a small bowl. Set aside.

3. Add peas, celery, scallion, and shrimp to cooked rice. Stir. Add about half of the dressing and stir to coat. If desired, add additional dressing to taste and stir. Salt and pepper to taste.

4. Serve warm or chilled.

Serves 8 to 10

COOK'S NOTES

COOK'S NOTES

OVEN-BAKED RICE

CAROL MENZ • MARSHALL FIELD'S

"This recipe was given to me by my sister-in-law in Ohio. It's excellent."

4 tablespoons butter, melted
1 10¾-ounce can condensed French onion soup
1 13¾-ounce can beef broth
1 7-ounce can mushroom stems and pieces, drained
1 cup brown rice
½ cup wild rice, rinsed
Garlic salt to taste
1 cup diced cooked steak or roast beef, if desired

1. Preheat oven to 375°F.
2. In a large mixing bowl, combine all ingredients. Transfer mixture to a 2-quart casserole dish. Cover and bake for about 1 hour, until all liquid has been absorbed and rice is tender.

Serves 8 to 10

WILD RICE STUFFING

SHIRLEY MOORE • MARSHALL FIELD'S

"This recipe came to me as I was planning our Thanksgiving dinner. It can be cooked in the bird or separately in a casserole, making it a delicious choice for vegetarian relatives and friends."

1 cup water
1 cup finely chopped celery
1 medium onion, chopped
1 14-ounce bag seasoned stuffing cubes
2 cups cooked wild rice
1 10¾-ounce can condensed cream of mushroom soup
1 cup chopped pecans
½ cup (1 stick) butter, melted
Salt and pepper to taste
1 14-ounce can artichokes packed in water,
    rinsed, drained, and chopped, if desired

1. Heat water to a boil. Add celery and onion and simmer until tender (about 10 minutes). Transfer mixture to a large bowl. Add remaining ingredients and mix well. (More water may be added if mixture seems too dry.)

2. Use to stuff a 12- to 15-pound turkey or transfer to a lightly greased casserole dish and bake at 350°F for about 1 hour.

Serves 10 to 12

COOK'S NOTES

ZUCCHINI "STUFFING" CASSEROLE

KARI SIEGEL • DAYTON'S

COOK'S NOTES

"My mother and I always anxiously await zucchini season so we can make and share this recipe. I'll gladly take anyone's extra zucchini to make this—try it and you will too!"

> 4 medium zucchini, sliced
> 1 10¾-ounce can condensed cream of chicken soup
> ½ cup sour cream
> ¾ cup shredded carrot
> ½ cup chopped onion
> ¼ teaspoon rubbed sage
> 2¼ cups sage- and onion-flavored stuffing cubes
> 2 cups (about ½ pound) shredded mozzarella cheese

1. Preheat oven to 350°F.

2. In a large pot, cook zucchini in boiling water until just tender (3 to 4 minutes). Drain well and transfer to a large mixing bowl. Add soup, sour cream, carrot, onion, sage, 2 cups of the stuffing mix, and 1¾ cups of the cheese. Mix well and place in a greased 2½-quart casserole. Sprinkle remaining ¼ cup stuffing mix and remaining ¼ cup cheese on top.

3. Bake for 30 to 35 minutes, until bubbly and browned on top.

Serves 4 to 6

SPOON BREAD CORN CASSEROLE

SHEILA HORST • MARSHALL FIELD'S

This recipe is from the collection of Genevieve Hall. "This is an easy-to-make crowd pleaser. It goes especially well with baked ham, and I love it with Cajun-grilled, extra thick pork chops."

> 1 cup (2 sticks) butter or margarine,
>   melted and cooled to room temperature
> 2 large eggs
> 1 14¾-ounce can cream-style corn
> 1 15¼-ounce can whole corn kernels, drained
> 1 8-ounce carton sour cream
> 1 8½-ounce package corn muffin mix

1. Preheat oven to 350°F.
2. In a large bowl, combine all ingredients. Mix thoroughly. Transfer to a 9″ × 11″ × 2″ casserole. Bake for about 40 minutes, until lightly browned.

Serves 10 to 12

VARIATION
Mexican-style whole corn kernels may be used.

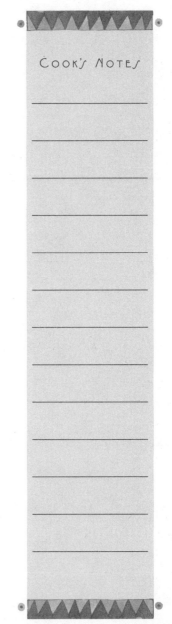

COOK'S NOTES

SWEDISH BROWN BREAD

BARBARA BAYLEY • DAYTON'S

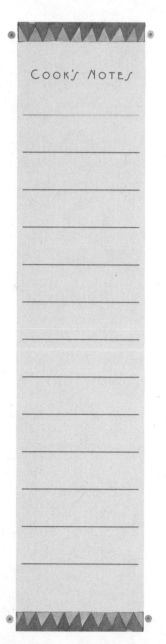

"In the early 1900s my grandmother baked this brown bread (it's actually rye bread) to sell at church. She used to bring 2 or 3 loaves to our home every week. As time went by, my mother and then I began making the bread, and I've passed this recipe down to my daughter-in-law."

1 ¼-ounce envelope active dry yeast
½ cup packed light brown sugar
¼ cup warm water (105°F to 115°F)
6 to 7 cups bread flour or all-purpose flour,
    plus flour for board
½ cup molasses
6 tablespoons vegetable oil
1½ teaspoons salt
1½ cups cold water
1 cup rye flour

1. In a glass, stir yeast and ½ teaspoon brown sugar into warm water. Let stand until foamy (about 10 minutes).

2. In a small saucepan, combine molasses, oil, salt, remaining brown sugar, and ½ cup cold water. Cook over medium heat until mixture is hot but not boiling. Transfer to a large bowl and mix in rye flour. Add yeast mixture and remaining 1 cup cold water. Mix to make a batter. Add 6 cups white flour and stir to form a dough. Dough should be soft but not sticky. Stir in more flour as needed.

3. Turn dough out onto a floured board. Knead until dough is smooth, supple, and elastic (about 8 minutes). Transfer to a medium greased bowl, cover, and let rise until dough has doubled in bulk (2½ to 3 hours). Punch dough down.

4. Divide dough in half. Shape each half into a loaf and place in greased 9″ × 5″ × 3″ loaf pans. Cover loosely and let rise until doubled in bulk (about 1 hour).

5. When dough has almost doubled, preheat oven to 325°F.

6. When dough has doubled, bake loaves for 50 to 60 minutes, until nicely browned. (They should sound hollow when rapped on the bottom.) Invert onto a cooling rack and let cool completely.

Makes 2 loaves

COOK'S NOTES

NANA TULLY'S IRISH SODA BREAD

LOUISE McNAMARA • DAYTON'S

"I used to love to watch my Irish grandmother make this bread from memory— she never used a recipe. One day I wrote down the ingredients and steps, and now her great-grandchildren enjoy eating this."

> 4 tablespoons butter or margarine, melted
> 4 cups all-purpose flour, plus flour for board
> 4½ teaspoons baking powder
> 2 tablespoons caraway seeds
> Pinch salt
> 3 tablespoons sugar
> 1¾ cups milk
> ½ teaspoon vanilla extract
> 1½ cup dark raisins

1. Preheat oven to 425°F.

2. Pour 3 tablespoons of the butter into an 8-inch round baking dish. Swirl to coat. Pour off excess butter into a medium bowl and set aside.

3. In a large bowl, combine flour, baking powder, caraway seeds, salt, and 2 tablespoons of the sugar. In the medium bowl, combine milk, vanilla, and remaining tablespoon melted butter.

4. Make a well in the center of the dry ingredients and pour in milk mixture. Stir to form a dough. Add raisins and mix well. Turn dough out onto a floured board. Knead lightly for about 1 minute, adding more flour if needed to keep dough from sticking. Shape into a ball and transfer to baking dish. Using your thumb, make a 1-inch-deep indentation in the center of the loaf.

5. Bake for 10 minutes. Reduce heat to 350°F and bake for 30 minutes more. Reduce heat to 325°F and bake until loaf is deep brown (20 to 30 minutes more). Invert onto a cooling rack, remove dish, and brush with remaining 1 tablespoon melted butter and remaining 1 tablespoon sugar.

Makes 1 loaf

COOK'S NOTES

COOK'S NOTES

OATMEAL BREAD

DR. JOHN S. LONG • MARSHALL FIELD'S

"This recipe has been in my family for three generations. It's nutritious and very tasty, especially when toasted."

> 2 cups hot water
> 1 cup old-fashioned rolled oats
> ¼ cup granulated sugar
> ¼ cup packed dark brown sugar or honey
> 2 tablespoons butter, margarine, or solid vegetable shortening
> 1½ teaspoons salt
> ½ cup warm water (105°F to 115°F)
> 1 ¼-ounce envelope active dry yeast
> 5 to 6 cups bread flour or all-purpose flour, plus flour for board

1. In a large bowl, combine hot water, oats, granulated sugar, brown sugar, butter, and salt. Stir well and let stand until cool.

2. Place warm water in a small glass. Sprinkle yeast over top and let stand until it begins to froth (about 5 minutes). Add to oat mixture. Add 5 cups of the flour and stir to form a dough. Dough should be soft but not sticky. Stir in more flour if needed.

3. Turn dough out onto a floured board and knead until smooth, supple, and elastic (about 8 minutes). Transfer to a medium greased bowl, cover, and let rise until dough has doubled in bulk (about 1½ hours).

4. Punch dough down and knead to remove air pockets. Divide dough in half and shape each half into a loaf. Transfer each to a greased 9″ × 5″ × 3″ loaf pan, cover, and let rise until doubled in bulk (about 1 hour).

5. When loaves have almost doubled, preheat oven to 375°F.

6. When loaves have doubled, bake for 35 to 45 minutes, until nicely browned. (They should sound hollow when rapped on the bottom.) Invert onto a cooling rack and let cool completely.

Makes 2 loaves

COOK'S NOTES

NANA'S BREAD

LIBBY FRANCO WEIL • DAYTON'S

"My grandmother, Virginia Franco, brought this recipe with her when she emigrated from Italy at age 21 to join her father in the United States. She cooked by instinct, never measuring ingredients exactly. When my mom wanted to get a more structured recipe for this bread, she worked alongside my grandmother and measured things as they went. It took a few tries to get it all down on paper!"

1½ cups warm water (105°F to 115°F)
2 ¼-ounce envelopes active dry yeast
½ cup (1 stick) butter or margarine, melted
1 cup vegetable oil
9 large eggs
1¼ cups sugar
1 teaspoon salt
Juice of 3 small lemons
Zest of 3 small lemons, grated coarse
4 pounds (about 10½ cups) all-purpose flour
1 large egg yolk, beaten

1. Place water in a small bowl. Stir in yeast. Let stand until it begins to froth (about 5 minutes).

2. In a small bowl, mix melted butter with oil.

3. Using an electric stand mixer fitted with paddle attachment, beat eggs, sugar, and salt at medium speed until mixture has thickened slightly. Beat in butter mixture, lemon juice, and lemon zest. Beat in 3 cups flour until incorporated. Beat in half of the yeast mixture. Beat in 3 cups flour, then remaining yeast, then 3 more cups flour.

4. Fit mixer with bread hook. Beat in remaining flour ½ cup at a time at medium speed until no longer sticky. Beat for about 10 minutes, until dough is smooth, supple, and elastic.

5. Place dough in a medium greased bowl, cover loosely, and leave in a warm place to rise overnight.

6. Punch down dough. Divide dough into quarters and place each quarter in a greased 9″ × 5″ × 3″ loaf pan. Place 4 sheets of wax paper that have been lightly sprayed with vegetable oil spray, oil side down, over loaves. Set aside in a warm place for 1¼ to 1½ hours, until loaves have doubled in size.

7. Preheat oven to 350°F.

8. Brush tops of loaves with beaten egg yolk. Bake for about 40 minutes, until crusts are golden brown and loaves sound hollow when tapped.

Makes 4 loaves

COOK'S NOTES

COOK'S NOTES

AUNT NETTIE'S KUGEL

SHEILA GERSHMAN • MARSHALL FIELD'S

"I believe my aunt began making this recipe in the 1950s. It's been on our dinner table for all kinds of holidays, but it's traditionally served at the Jewish New Year. It's a treat."

> 1 pound broad egg noodles
> 8 large eggs, beaten
> 2 cups milk
> 1 cup sugar
> 1 cup (2 sticks) butter, melted and cooled to room temperature
> 1 pound whipped cream cheese at room temperature
> 1 cup crushed cornflakes, if desired

1. Preheat oven to 350°F.

2. Cook noodles according to package directions. Drain and place noodles in a large mixing bowl. Add eggs, milk, sugar, butter, and cream cheese. Mix well. Pour into an 11⅝″ × 9¼″ × 2½″ aluminum foil pan. If desired, sprinkle crushed cornflakes on top.

3. Bake until firm and browned on top (1 to 1¼ hours).

Serves 16

GRAMA'S APPLE CRISP

SALLY BLAIR • DAYTON'S

"I have such fond memories of my dear grandmother baking this wonderful treat. This was the first recipe she taught me after I was married in 1956."

6 to 8 small apples, peeled and cored
¼ cup water
1½ teaspoons ground cinnamon
Pinch salt
1 cup sugar
¾ cup all-purpose flour
⅓ cup butter, plus butter to grease pie plate
Garnish: Whipped cream or ice cream for serving

1. Preheat oven to 350°F.

2. Butter a 9- to 10-inch pie plate. Cut apples into ½-inch slices and place in pie plate. Pour water over apples and sprinkle with half of the cinnamon and a small pinch of salt.

3. Make the topping. Using a pastry blender, mix together sugar, flour, butter, and remaining cinnamon until butter is cut to the size of small peas. Sprinkle over apples and, using your hands, pat down lightly.

4. Place pie plate on a foil-lined baking sheet. Bake for 45 to 50 minutes, until apples are tender and top is nicely browned. Serve warm with whipped cream or ice cream.

Serves 6

COOK'S NOTES

PEACH COBBLER

MINNEAPOLIS MAYOR SHARON SAYLES BELTON • DAYTON'S

"Family and friends all know this is one of my favorite desserts."

> 8 cups sliced fresh peaches (6 to 8 peaches)
> 2 cups sugar
> ¼ cup all-purpose flour
> ½ teaspoon ground nutmeg
> 1 teaspoon almond extract
> 5 tablespoons plus 1 teaspoon butter or margarine
> 2 prepared refrigerated piecrusts

1. Preheat oven to 425°F.

2. In a Dutch oven, combine peaches, sugar, flour, and nutmeg. Set aside for about 5 minutes, until a syrup forms. Bring to a boil over medium heat. Reduce heat to low and simmer for 10 minutes, stirring occasionally. Remove from heat. Add almond extract. Add butter or margarine and stir until melted.

3. On a lightly floured work surface, roll 1 piecrust out until ⅛ inch thick. Trim to an 8-inch square. Place half of the peach mixture into a lightly greased 8-inch square baking pan. Top with pastry square. Bake for about 15 minutes, until lightly browned.

4. While peach mixture is baking, roll remaining piecrust out until ⅛ inch thick. Trim to an 8-inch square and cut into 8 1-inch-wide strips. Place remaining peach mixture onto partially baked cobbler. Arrange pastry strips in a lattice design on top. Bake for 15 to 20 minutes more, until strips are lightly browned.

Serves 6 to 8

COOK'S NOTES

RHUBARB PIE

JULIANNE NYBERG • DAYTON'S

"My mother, Mildred G. Fandel, was, in my opinion, the fastest and best pie maker in my hometown of Ladysmith, Wisconsin. She always made her pies for visitors and for fund-raisers. Before she passed away in 1986, she shared this special seasonal recipe with me and my seven sisters."

*1 pound rhubarb, trimmed and cut into
    1-inch chunks (about 3 cups)*
2 prepared 9-inch pie shells
1½ cups sugar
3 tablespoons all-purpose flour
½ teaspoon ground nutmeg
1 tablespoon butter
3 large eggs

1. Preheat oven to 450°F.

2. Place rhubarb in one of the piecrusts. In a medium bowl, combine sugar, flour, and nutmeg. Using a knife or a pastry blender, cut in butter. Beat 2 of the eggs and stir in until incorporated. Pour over rhubarb.

3. Cover rhubarb with remaining piecrust and brush with remaining egg, beaten. Bake for 10 minutes. Reduce heat to 350°F and bake for about 40 minutes more, until crust is golden. Cool on a cooling rack.

Serves 6 to 8

COOK'S NOTES

LEMON MERINGUE PIE

DOROTHY FALKENBERG • MARSHALL FIELD'S

"This was the favorite dessert of my mother, Dorothea Falkenberg, and many of my childhood friends from the 1950s and '40s remember it with fondness. The taste of it always brings back loving memories of my mother."

3 tablespoons cornstarch
1 cup granulated sugar
1 cup boiling water
2 tablespoons butter
Zest of ½ medium lemon, grated
Juice of 1 medium lemon plus
  1 teaspoon

1 medium egg, beaten
1 9" prepared piecrust
2 medium egg whites, at room
  temperature
2 tablespoons confectioners' sugar
¼ teaspoon cream of tartar

1. Preheat oven to 350°F.

2. In a saucepan, mix cornstarch with granulated sugar and boiling water. Boil for 5 minutes. Whisk in butter, lemon zest, juice of 1 lemon, and beaten egg. Pour mixture into piecrust. Bake for 25 to 35 minutes, until crust is browned. Remove from oven and let cool on a rack.

3. Preheat broiler.

4. Using an electric mixer, beat egg whites on high speed until frothy. Add confectioners' sugar, 1 teaspoon lemon juice, and cream of tartar and continue to beat until peaks form and meringue appears glossy. Pile meringue on top of pie. Place pie in broiler 2 to 3 inches from the heat source for 1 to 2 minutes, until meringue peaks turn light brown. Do not burn.

Serves 6 to 8

FROSTY LIME PIE

EDITH CAHN • MARSHALL FIELD'S

"This pie is simple to make and very refreshing to eat. I make this several times a year, including St. Patrick's Day. My friends often ask for it."

1¼ cups applesauce
½ cup sugar
1 3-ounce package lime-flavored gelatin
1 small can (⅔ cup) evaporated milk
1 tablespoon lemon or lime juice
1 prepared graham cracker crust

1. In a small saucepan, combine applesauce, sugar, and gelatin over medium heat. Bring to a boil and cook, stirring constantly, until sugar and gelatin are completely dissolved. Remove from heat and refrigerate until mixture is almost set.

2. Using an electric mixer, whip evaporated milk until soft peaks form. Gently fold gelatin mixture into whipped milk. Fold in lemon or lime juice.

3. Pour mixture into piecrust. Refrigerate for at least 1 hour before serving.

Serves 6 to 8

COOK'S NOTES

FROZEN LEMON PIE

CINDY BAUBIE • DAYTON'S

"This easy dessert has been handed down to me from my mom, Dorothy Osborne, who received it from her aunt, Edith Luse. Every time I serve it to guests, someone always remarks how this brings back memories of childhood."

¾ cup crushed vanilla wafers
3 large eggs, separated
¼ cup fresh lemon juice
Zest of ½ lemon, grated

⅛ teaspoon salt
½ cup plus 1 tablespoon sugar
1 cup heavy cream, whipped

1. Press half of the crushed wafers evenly into the bottom of a 9″ × 5″ × 3″ loaf pan. Set aside.

2. In a small bowl, lightly beat egg yolks. Bring water in the bottom of a double boiler to a simmer. Place yolks, lemon juice, lemon zest, salt, and sugar in the top of the double boiler and cook for 6 to 8 minutes, stirring constantly, until thick. Remove from heat and let cool.

3. Transfer custard to a medium bowl. Wash and dry the top part of the double boiler. Bring the water to a simmer. Place egg whites in the top, making sure that the water doesn't touch the bottom of the insert. Using an electric mixer, beat until soft peaks form (about 4 minutes).

4. Fold egg whites into lemon custard. Fold in whipped cream. Pour mixture into loaf pan. Cover with remaining crushed wafers. Cover with plastic wrap and freeze until firm (at least 1 hour). Remove pan from freezer, invert onto a platter, and slice.

Serves 6 to 8

RASPBERRY ICE CREAM PIE

KATHRYN REUTZEL • DAYTON'S

"This was my family's favorite summer dessert. We'd make it as soon as the first berries of the season appeared. It always made a hot, humid day seem cooler."

CRUST

> 1½ cups graham cracker crumbs
> ⅓ cup melted butter
> 2 tablespoons sugar

FILLING

> 1 3-ounce package raspberry flavored gelatin
> 1 cup boiling water
> 1 pint vanilla ice cream
> 1 cup fresh raspberries
> Garnish: additional raspberries, if desired

1. Preheat oven to 350°F.

2. Make the crust. In a mixing bowl, combine graham cracker crumbs, butter, and sugar. Press evenly into the bottom and sides of a 9-inch pie plate. Bake for 8 to 10 minutes, until set. Let cool completely before filling.

3. Make the filling. In a large bowl, combine gelatin and boiling water, stirring until gelatin has dissolved completely (about 2 minutes). Add ice cream and stir until ice cream is melted and mixture is smooth. Refrigerate until mixture thickens but is still pourable.

4. Spread 1 cup berries over piecrust. Pour filling over berries. If desired, garnish top with additional berries. Refrigerate until set (1 to 2 hours).

Serves 6 to 8

COOK'S NOTES

BUTTERSCOTCH PIE

MYRNA JOHNSON • DAYTON'S

"My children always wanted this butterscotch pie instead of birthday cake on their special day. This recipe was handed down to me by my mother. Compared to many desserts, this is a very inexpensive indulgence."

FILLING

1½ cups packed light brown sugar
¼ cup all-purpose flour
1½ cups cold water
2 large egg yolks, lightly beaten
1 tablespoon butter or margarine
1 tablespoon vanilla extract
1 9-inch prebaked pie shell

MERINGUE

3 large egg whites, at room temperature
3 tablespoons granulated sugar
1 tablespoon vanilla extract
Pinch salt

1. Make the filling. In a medium saucepan, combine brown sugar and flour, stirring well. Add water and heat to a boil over medium heat. Reduce heat to low and, whisking constantly, gradually add egg yolks. Cook, stirring constantly, until mixture thickens (about 4 to 5 minutes). Remove from heat and add butter and vanilla. Stir until smooth.

2. Pour mixture into pie shell and let cool to room temperature.

3. Preheat the oven to 350°F.

4. Make the meringue. Using an electric mixer, beat egg whites on high speed until foamy. Beating constantly, gradually add granulated sugar. Continue to beat until whites are thick and glossy and form peaks. Add vanilla and salt and mix well.

5. Spread meringue over pie. Bake for 5 to 8 minutes, until meringue begins to brown at edges. Let cool before serving.

Serves 6 to 8

COOK'S NOTES

BRANDY ALEXANDER PIE

MADLYN DANIEL • MARSHALL FIELD'S

"This dessert is much better when made a day or two ahead of time. Allowing the flavors to mingle overnight really brings out the best in this recipe."

> 1 ¼-ounce envelope unflavored gelatin
> ½ cup cold water
> ⅛ teaspoon salt
> 3 eggs, separated
> ⅔ cup sugar
> ¼ cup cognac
> ¼ cup crème de cacao
> ¼ tablespoon cream of tartar
> 2 cups heavy cream, whipped
> 1 9-inch prepared graham cracker crust
> Garnish: chocolate curls (See Note)

1. In a small saucepan, sprinkle gelatin over cold water. Add salt, egg yolks, and ⅓ cup of the sugar. Stir well. Heat over low heat, stirring constantly, until gelatin dissolves (about 5 minutes). Remove from heat.

2. Stir in cognac and crème de cacao. Refrigerate until mixture thickens but has not set (about 1 hour).

3. Bring water to a simmer in the bottom of a double boiler. Place egg whites in the top, making sure the water doesn't bubble up enough to touch the bottom of the insert. Using an electric mixer, beat until soft peaks form (about 4 minutes).

4. Fold egg whites into gelatin mixture. Fold in 1 cup whipped cream. Pour into pie shell. Refrigerate overnight.

5. Garnish with chocolate curls and remaining 1 cup whipped cream.

Serves 6 to 8

NOTE

To make chocolate curls, run a vegetable peeler firmly but gently along the side of a block of sweetened chocolate (block should be at least 3 inches long).

COOK'S NOTES

CHOCOLATE ECLAIR "PIE"

JOAN DEUTSCH • DAYTON'S

"This recipe was given to me by a very dear neighbor. She's 85 years old and fit as a fiddle. We enjoy playing cards together."

PIE

> 36 5" × 2½" graham crackers
> 2 3-ounce packages French vanilla instant pudding mix
> 3 cups milk
> 1 8-ounce container frozen nondairy dessert topping

FROSTING

> 2 ounces (¼ cup) chocolate syrup
> 3 tablespoons milk
> 2 tablespoons butter
> 3 tablespoons white corn syrup
> 2 teaspoons vanilla extract
> 1½ cups confectioners' sugar

1. Make the pie. Line a 9" × 13" pan with 12 whole graham crackers. Set aside.

2. In a medium bowl, combine pudding mix and milk. Blend until thick. Fold in dessert topping.

3. Pour half of mixture into pan. Top with a layer of 12 graham crackers. Pour remaining mixture over graham crackers. Top with remaining 12 graham crackers.

4. Make the frosting. In a microwave-safe dish or a saucepan, combine chocolate syrup, milk, butter, corn syrup, and vanilla extract. Heat in microwave oven on high for 15 seconds or until butter is melted or, if using a saucepan, heat over low heat for 3 to 5 minutes. Remove from heat. Beat in confectioners' sugar.

5. Frost top of pie. Refrigerate for at least 24 hours before serving.

Serves 18

COOK'S NOTES

MIMI'S PLUM KUCHEN

PAMELA DEGENER BENZ • MARSHALL FIELD'S

"Although this sounds like a German recipe (with Italian plums!), it comes from my Irish-Dutch grandmother, who used to make it for her family in the 1930s and '40s. My mother passed the recipe to me when I was a teenager. It is the one dessert my cholesterol-conscious husband requests each year."

KUCHEN

> 1 cup all-purpose flour
> 1 teaspoon baking powder
> ½ teaspoon salt
> ½ cup (1 stick) unsalted butter, at room temperature
> ½ cup sugar
> 2 large eggs, beaten
> ½ teaspoon almond extract
> 10 to 12 Italian prune plums,
>   halved lengthwise and pitted (see Note)

TOPPING

> ½ cup sugar
> 1 teaspoon ground cinnamon
> Garnish: almond extract–flavored whipped cream

1. Make the kuchen. Preheat oven to 400°F.

2. In a medium bowl, sift together flour, baking powder, and salt. Set aside.

COOK'S NOTES

3. Place butter and sugar in a large bowl and, using an electric mixer at medium speed, cream. Add beaten eggs and mix thoroughly. Gently fold flour mixture into creamed mixture. Stir in almond extract.

4. Place batter in a lightly greased 9-inch round cake pan. Press plums onto batter, skin side down.

5. Make the topping. In a small bowl, combine sugar and cinnamon. Sprinkle over plums.

6. Place pan on the middle rack of the oven. Bake for about 30 minutes, until topping is bubbly and a tester inserted into the kuchen comes out clean. Transfer to a cooling rack and let cool.

7. Serve warm or cold, with almond extract–flavored whipped cream.

Serves 6 to 8

NOTE

Blue Italian prune plums are available seasonally (usually in late June or early July).

COOK'S NOTES

PUMPKIN CHEESECAKE

URSULA MAURER • MARSHALL FIELD'S

"As an alternative to pumpkin pie, I developed this recipe for special occasions after tasting a similar cheesecake at a restaurant. The maple-flavored topping gives it a Wisconsin touch."

CRUST

1¼ cups graham cracker crumbs
5 tablespoons plus 1 teaspoon unsalted butter, melted
¼ cup packed light brown sugar
1 teaspoon ground cinnamon

FILLING

2 8-ounce packages cream cheese, at room temperature
16 ounces Neufchâtel cheese at room temperature
1¾ cups granulated sugar
3 large egg yolks
⅓ cup heavy cream
1½ cups canned pumpkin puree
2 teaspoons ground cinnamon

TOPPING

1 cup sour cream
2 tablespoons sugar
1 tablespoon pure maple syrup

1. Make the crust. In a mixing bowl, combine all ingredients. Mix thoroughly. Press evenly into the bottom of a 9-inch springform pan, working mixture 1½ inches up the sides of the pan. Refrigerate for 30 minutes.

2. Preheat the oven to 300°F.

3. Make the filling. Place cheeses and sugar in a large bowl. Using an electric mixer, cream. Add egg yolks and cream and continue beating until smooth. Add pumpkin and cinnamon. Beat until completely blended.

4. Pour filling into chilled crust. Bake for 1½ hours (do not open the oven door while baking). Turn off oven and let cake sit for 1 hour more with the oven door closed. Remove from oven.

5. Heat oven to 325°F.

6. Make the topping. In a mixing bowl, combine sour cream, sugar, and maple syrup. Blend thoroughly and spread over cake. Return cake to oven and bake for 10 minutes.

7. Remove from oven and let cool on a cooling rack for 2 to 3 hours, until cake is at room temperature. Refrigerate overnight before removing sides of springform pan.

Serves 16

COOK'S NOTES

GRAND MARNIER CHEESECAKE

Barbara A. Duchene • Hudson's

"This is an incredibly luscious dessert. Everyone loves the combined flavors of the orange zest and the oatmeal-raisin cookies, and the Grand Marnier gives the cheesecake an extra-special touch."

CRUST

> 2½ cups crushed oatmeal-raisin cookies
> ½ cup (1 stick) unsalted butter, melted

FILLING

> 4 8-ounce packages cream cheese, at room temperature
> ½ cup sugar
> 2 tablespoons all-purpose flour
> 5 large eggs, at room temperature
> ½ cup sour cream
> 2 teaspoons finely chopped orange zest
> ½ teaspoon salt
> ½ tablespoon vanilla extract
> ⅓ cup Grand Marnier liqueur
> Garnish: white and dark chocolate curls (see Note),
>   or mandarin orange sections, if desired

1. Make the crust. Combine cookie crumbs and butter. Mix thoroughly and press in an even layer on the bottom of a 10-inch springform pan. Refrigerate for 30 minutes.

2. Preheat oven to 325°F.

3. Make the filling. Using an electric mixer, cream together cream cheese and sugar. Mix in flour. Add eggs one at a time, beating well after each addition. Scrape down sides of the bowl.

4. Add sour cream, orange zest, salt, vanilla, and liqueur and mix thoroughly. Pour mixture over crust in the pan.

5. Line a large baking sheet with aluminum foil. Place springform pan on baking sheet and place in the oven. Bake for 70 minutes.

6. Turn the oven off. Let cake cool in the oven for 1 hour (do not open the oven door). Remove from oven and let cool at room temperature for 2 to 3 hours. Refrigerate for 8 hours or overnight.

7. Remove sides of pan and transfer cheesecake to a serving platter. Garnish with white and dark chocolate curls or with mandarin oranges.

Serves 12 to 16

NOTE

To make chocolate curls, run a vegetable peeler gently but firmly along a block of sweetened chocolate (block should be at least 3 inches long).

COOK'S NOTES

FLUFFY CHEESECAKE

ROSEANN CORALLO • HUDSON'S

"This is the perfect cheesecake—delicious and incredibly easy to make."

COOK'S NOTES

4 large eggs
15 ounces (about 2 cups) ricotta cheese
2 8-ounce packages cream cheese, at room temperature
½ cup (1 stick) butter or margarine, melted
2 teaspoons vanilla extract
3 tablespoons all-purpose flour
3 tablespoons cornstarch
1½ cups sugar
1 16-ounce container sour cream
Garnish: sliced strawberries, blueberries, or
    hot fudge sauce, if desired

1. Preheat oven to 350°F.

2. In a large mixing bowl, lightly beat eggs. Add ricotta cheese, cream cheese, butter or margarine, and vanilla. Using an electric mixer at low speed, beat until smooth. Add flour, cornstarch, and sugar. Mix until incorporated. Fold in sour cream.

3. Pour batter into a greased 10-inch springform pan. Bake for 45 minutes. Turn off oven and let cake cool in the oven for 2 hours. Refrigerate for at least 4 hours. Garnish with sliced strawberries, blueberries, or hot fudge sauce, if desired.

Serves 12

HAPPY APPLE CAKE

SANDRA KORT • HUDSON'S

"This recipe has been in our family for about 25 years. Everyone raves about it—it's versatile, easy to make, and delicious."

5 McIntosh apples
1 teaspoon ground cinnamon
1½ cups plus 5 tablespoons sugar
3 cups all-purpose flour
½ teaspoon salt
4 large eggs, well beaten

1 cup vegetable oil
⅓ cup orange juice
2 teaspoons vanilla extract
½ teaspoon baking soda
½ teaspoon baking powder

1. Preheat oven to 350°F.

2. Peel, core, and thinly slice apples. In a large bowl, toss apples in cinnamon and 5 tablespoons sugar. Set aside.

3. In a large mixing bowl, combine flour, salt, and remaining 1½ cups sugar. Add eggs, oil, orange juice, and vanilla. Using an electric mixer, beat at low speed just until ingredients are incorporated. Beat at high speed until well-blended (about 2 minutes). Add baking soda and baking powder. Blend at high speed for 2 minutes more.

4. Coat bottom of a buttered and floured tube pan with 1⅔ cups batter, spreading batter evenly with a rubber spatula. Arrange 1⅔ cups apple mixture in a thin layer over batter. Repeat process twice. Bake for 1 hour, until a tester inserted in center of cake comes out clean and cake has pulled away from sides of the pan. Let cool.

Serves 12 to 16

COOK'S NOTES

RHUBARB DESSERT CAKE

Joyce Peltz • Dayton's

"It's a family tradition to make this cake for Mother's Day dinner, using fresh rhubarb from the garden."

CAKE

> 4 tablespoons butter at room temperature
> 1 cup granulated sugar
> 1 large egg
> 2 tablespoons hot water
> 1 teaspoon vanilla extract
> 1 cup all-purpose flour
> 1 teaspoon baking soda
> ¼ teaspoon salt
> 1 teaspoon ground cinnamon
> 1 scant teaspoon ground nutmeg
> 2½ cups (about 1 pound) trimmed and cubed rhubarb
> ½ cup chopped walnuts

CARAMEL SAUCE

> ½ cup (1 stick) butter
> ½ cup granulated sugar
> ½ cup packed light brown sugar
> 1 tablespoon all-purpose flour
> ½ cup heavy cream
> 1 teaspoon vanilla extract

COOK'S NOTES

1. Preheat oven to 350°F.

2. Make the cake. Place butter and sugar in a large bowl. Using an electric mixer at low speed, cream. Mix in egg, hot water, and vanilla. Sift flour, baking soda, salt, cinnamon, and nutmeg together into mixture and mix in. Fold in rhubarb and nuts.

3. Pour batter into a greased and lightly floured 9-inch round cake pan and bake for about 45 minutes, until a tester inserted in center of cake comes out clean. Cool in pan on a cooling rack.

4. Make the sauce. In a small saucepan, combine butter, sugar, brown sugar, flour, and cream. Bring to a boil over medium heat. Boil for 3 to 5 minutes, stirring constantly, until thick enough to coat the back of a spoon. Remove from heat and stir in vanilla. Serve sauce warm over cake.

Serves 6 to 8

COOK'S NOTES

RAISIN SPICE CAKE

MARY JANE O'CONNELL • MARSHALL FIELD'S

"This recipe has been a favorite of my grandmother and her family, my mother and our family, and now my own family of 5 children and 13 grandchildren."

1¾ cups sifted all-purpose flour
1 teaspoon baking soda
1 teaspoon ground allspice
1 teaspoon ground cinnamon
1 teaspoon ground nutmeg
1 teaspoon ground cloves

1 cup dark raisins
2 cups water
½ cup (1 stick) butter or margarine
1 cup sugar
1 large egg, lightly beaten

1. Preheat oven to 350°F.

2. Grease and flour a 9″ × 5″ × 3″ loaf pan and set aside. In a large bowl, sift together flour, baking soda, and spices. Set aside.

3. In a saucepan, combine raisins and water. Boil for 10 minutes. Remove from heat and add butter or margarine. Set aside until mixture has cooled to lukewarm. Add sugar and egg to raisin mixture and mix well. Add to flour mixture and stir to combine.

4. Place batter in pan and bake for 35 to 40 minutes, until a toothpick inserted in center comes out clean. Cool in pan for 5 minutes. Using a small knife, loosen cake from sides of pan and invert onto a cooling rack to cool completely.

Serves 8 to 10

BANANA BREAD

BONNIE NAGLE • DAYTON'S

"This recipe was given to me by my mother. I can remember walking home from school, smelling the aroma of this bread as I walked up the path (the 'bunny trail,' as we kids called it) home."

> 2 teaspoons baking soda
> 1 cup buttermilk
> 1½ cups (3 sticks) butter or margarine
> 3 cups sugar
> 4 large eggs
> 3 cups (6 to 7 large) mashed banana
> 2 teaspoons vanilla extract
> 4 cups all-purpose flour
> 2 teaspoons salt
> 1 cup chopped walnuts or chocolate chips, if desired

1. Preheat oven to 350°F.

2. In a small bowl, dissolve baking soda in buttermilk. Set aside.

3. Place butter or margarine and sugar in a large bowl. Using an electric mixer at low speed, cream. Beat in eggs. Beat in bananas and vanilla. Add flour and salt. Add buttermilk mixture. Add nuts or chocolate chips, if desired. Using a wooden spoon, mix just until ingredients are incorporated.

4. Pour equal amounts of batter into 4 greased 9″ × 5″ × 3″ loaf pans. Bake for 1 hour, until a toothpick inserted in center of each loaf comes out clean. Transfer to a cooling rack and let cool.

Makes 4 loaves

COOK'S NOTES

AUNT GRACE'S HOOSIER COFFEE CAKE

MARY C. BRAUN • MARSHALL FIELD'S

"Aunt Grace served this coffee cake whenever we visited her. It always made us feel welcome. Now it's my turn to welcome company with this delicious recipe."

2½ cups sifted cake flour
1 teaspoon baking powder
¼ teaspoon salt
1 cup butter, softened, plus 1 tablespoon, melted
2 cups granulated sugar
2 large eggs
1 cup sour cream
½ teaspoon vanilla extract
¾ cup packed light brown sugar
½ cup chopped walnuts
1 teaspoon ground cinnamon

1. Preheat oven to 350°F.

2. In a medium bowl, sift together flour, baking powder, and salt. Set aside.

3. Place softened butter and granulated sugar in a large bowl. Using an electric mixer at medium speed, cream until light and fluffy (about 2 minutes). Add eggs one at a time, mixing well after each addition. Mix in sour cream and vanilla. Add flour mixture and, using a rubber spatula, mix.

4. In a small bowl, combine brown sugar, walnuts, cinnamon, and melted butter.

5. Spoon half of batter into a greased 10-inch bundt pan. Sprinkle half of walnut mixture over batter. Top with remaining batter. Sprinkle remaining walnut mixture over batter.

6. Bake for 55 to 60 minutes, until a toothpick inserted in center of cake comes out clean. Let cool in pan for 5 minutes. Invert onto a cooling rack and let cool completely.

Serves 10 to 12

COOK'S NOTES

G. G.'S (GREAT-GRANDMA'S) CHOCOLATE CHIP CAKE

SUE FRIEDMAN • DAYTON'S

"Grandma Shirley Rait celebrated her 90th birthday this year. She still bakes this cake, and all of her grandchildren and her great-grandchildren think it's the best dessert in the world."

CAKE

> 2 cups cake flour
> 1 teaspoon baking powder
> 1 teaspoon baking soda
> ½ cup (1 stick) butter, at room temperature
> 1 cup sugar
> 2 large eggs, at room temperature
> 2 cups sour cream
> 1 teaspoon vanilla extract

TOPPING

> ¾ cup chocolate chips
> ¾ cup chopped walnuts
> ⅓ cup sugar
> 1 teaspoon cinnamon

1. Preheat oven to 350°F.

2. Make the cake. Sift together flour, baking powder, and baking soda. Set aside.

3. Using an electric mixer on high speed, beat together butter and sugar until light and fluffy (3 to 4 minutes). Add eggs one at a time, beating well after each addition. Add sour cream and vanilla. Mix just until combined. Add flour mixture. Using a spatula, gently fold flour mixture into egg mixture. Transfer half of the batter to a lightly greased 10-inch bundt pan.

4. Make the topping. Mix together chocolate chips, walnuts, sugar, and cinnamon.

5. Sprinkle half of the topping over batter in the pan. Top with remaining batter, then remaining topping. Bake for 55 to 60 minutes, until a toothpick inserted in center of cake comes out clean.

6. Remove pan from oven. Let cool for 5 minutes, then invert onto a cooling rack and let cake cool completely (about 1 hour).

Serves 8 to 12

COOK'S NOTES

BUTTERMILK CHOCOLATE CAKE

VICKI HOLTAN • DAYTON'S

"I remember my childhood Saturday-morning routine of the kids cleaning our rooms and baking my dad's favorite recipe—this cake. Now, as a mother of 3, I don't bake this every Saturday, but I never miss the chance to make it for my parents when they come to visit. My dad still loves it, and I love baking it for him."

CAKE

> 2 cups all-purpose flour
> 2 teaspoons baking soda
> ½ teaspoon salt
> 6 rounded tablespoons unsweetened cocoa powder
> ½ cup solid vegetable shortening
> 2 cups sugar
> 2 large eggs
> 2 cups buttermilk
> 1 teaspoon vanilla extract

FROSTING

> ⅓ cup milk
> ¼ cup solid vegetable shortening
> 1 cup sugar
> 1 1-ounce square unsweetened chocolate
> 1 teaspoon vanilla extract

1. Preheat oven to 350°F.

2. Make the cake. In a large bowl, sift together flour, baking soda, salt, and cocoa powder. Set aside.

3. Place shortening and sugar in a large bowl. Using an electric mixer on medium speed, cream. Beat in eggs until mixture is light and creamy. Add flour mixture, buttermilk, and vanilla. Mix well.

4. Pour batter into a 9″ × 13″ baking pan that has been greased and lightly floured, and bake for 45 to 50 minutes, until a toothpick inserted in center of cake comes out clean. Transfer to a cooling rack and let cool in pan.

5. Make the frosting. In a saucepan, combine milk, shortening, sugar, and chocolate. Bring to a boil over medium heat and boil for 1 minute, stirring constantly. Remove from heat and stir in vanilla. Beat by hand until frosting is smooth and creamy. Quickly spread over cooled cake.

Serves 12 to 16

COOK'S NOTES

FRANGO® CHOCOLATE SHEET CAKE

SUSAN KRAMER • DAYTON'S

"This recipe is quick and easy to make, and it's delicious. I make this for get-togethers with friends, and my husband often takes it to work. I'm sure it will become a favorite of many people."

CAKE

¾ cup (1½ sticks) butter or margarine
1 cup water
2 cups granulated sugar
2 cups all-purpose flour
2 tablespoons unsweetened cocoa powder
2 tablespoons Frango Mint Chocolate Cocoa, Frango Raspberry
  Chocolate Cocoa, or Frango Toffee Chocolate Cocoa
2 large eggs, lightly beaten
½ cup buttermilk
1½ teaspoons baking soda
1 teaspoon vanilla extract

FROSTING

4 tablespoons butter or margarine
¼ cup buttermilk
3 cups confectioners' sugar
2 tablespoons unsweetened cocoa powder
2 tablespoons Frango Mint Chocolate Cocoa, Frango Raspberry
  Chocolate Cocoa, or Frango Toffee Chocolate Cocoa
1 teaspoon vanilla extract

COOK'S NOTES

1. Preheat oven to 350°F.

2. Make the cake. In a large saucepan, combine butter and water. Bring to a boil. Remove from heat and set aside.

3. In a large bowl, stir together granulated sugar, flour, and cocoas. Add to butter mixture, stirring until smooth. Add eggs and mix well.

4. In a medium bowl, stir together buttermilk, baking soda, and vanilla. Add to batter and stir to combine.

5. Transfer batter to a greased jelly-roll pan and bake for 20 minutes, until center of cake is set (when a toothpick inserted into the center comes out clean). Transfer to a cooling rack and let cool in pan.

6. Make the frosting. In a saucepan, melt butter over medium heat. Remove pan from heat and stir in buttermilk. Stir in confectioners' sugar, cocoas, and vanilla. Quickly spread over slightly warm cake.

Serves 18 to 24

COOK'S NOTES

DIED-and-WENT-to-HEAVEN CHOCOLATE CAKE

MARLYS JOHNSON • DAYTON'S

"This is absolutely delicious, and it's easy to make, too."

> 1¾ cups all-purpose flour
> 1 cup granulated sugar
> 1 cup packed light brown sugar
> ¾ cup Dutch process cocoa powder
> 1½ teaspoons baking powder
> 1½ teaspoons baking soda
> ½ teaspoon salt
> 1¼ cups buttermilk
> ¼ cup vegetable oil
> 2 large eggs, lightly beaten
> 2 teaspoons vanilla extract
> 1 cup hot strong black coffee

1. Preheat oven to 350°F.

2. In a large bowl, combine flour, sugars, cocoa, baking powder, baking soda and salt. In a small bowl, combine buttermilk, oil, eggs, and vanilla. Add to flour mixture. Using an electric mixer on medium speed, mix until smooth (about 2 minutes). Whisk in coffee.

3. Pour batter into a greased and lightly floured bundt pan and bake for 35 to 40 minutes, until a toothpick inserted in center of cake comes out clean. Let cool in pan for 5 minutes. Invert onto a cooling rack and let cool.

Serves 10 to 12

VIENNA ALMOND TORTE

AUDREY E. PAUL • MARSHALL FIELD'S

"This was my grandmother's best recipe. I like more lemon flavor than she did, so I've adapted the recipe to include the zest of a large (instead of a small) lemon."

> 8 large eggs
> 1¾ cups granulated sugar
> ½ pound ground blanched almonds (2 cups)
> ¼ cup all-purpose flour
> Zest of 1 large lemon, grated
> Garnish: confectioners' sugar

1. Preheat oven to 325°F.

2. Line bottom of a lightly greased 10-inch tube pan with wax paper.

3. Separate 4 of the eggs. Set egg whites aside. Using a wooden spoon, beat together egg yolks, 4 whole eggs, and granulated sugar until thick and lemon colored (about 5 minutes). Stir in almonds, flour, and lemon zest.

4. Using an electric mixer, beat egg whites until stiff but not dry. Gently fold egg whites into batter. Place batter in pan and bake for 1 hour, until a toothpick inserted in center of torte comes out clean. Let cool completely in pan. Using a small knife, carefully loosen sides of pan. Invert onto a cooling rack. Place another rack on top of torte and invert again so torte is right side up. Just before serving, sift confectioners' sugar over top.

Serves 10 to 12

COOK'S NOTES

PUMPKIN MUFFINS

CHERYL ANDERSON • DAYTON'S

"This recipe has become a Thanksgiving tradition. It's also a much-requested favorite of my father, who says that pumpkin is good any time of the year."

½ cup dark raisins
¼ cup boiling water
1½ cups self-rising flour
1 cup sugar
½ teaspoon ground cinnamon
¼ teaspoon ground nutmeg
¾ cup vegetable oil
½ cup canned pumpkin puree
2 large eggs
½ cup chopped pecans or walnuts, if desired

1. Preheat oven to 350°F.

2. In a small bowl, combine raisins and boiling water. Set aside for 5 minutes to allow raisins to plump. Drain.

3. In a large bowl, mix together flour, sugar, cinnamon, and nutmeg. Add oil, pumpkin, and eggs. Mix just until ingredients are incorporated. Stir in raisins and, if desired, nuts.

4. Grease a 12-cup muffin tin or line with paper cup liners. Pour equal amounts batter into each cup and bake for 25 minutes, until tops are slightly browned. Let cool in tin on a cooling rack.

Makes 12 muffins

BISCOTTI DI ANISETTA

PAM SCHMIDT • MARSHALL FIELD'S

"My husband's grandmother, Calogera Grisafi, always made this recipe for special celebrations. 'Grandma' was born in 1894."

> 2 cups all-purpose flour
> 2 teaspoons baking powder
> ¼ teaspoon salt
> ½ cup (1 stick) butter, at room temperature
> 1 cup sugar
> 3 large eggs
> 3 drops anise oil

1. Preheat oven to 375°F.

2. In a medium bowl, sift together flour, baking powder, and salt. Set aside.

3. Place butter and sugar in a large bowl. Using an electric mixer on medium speed, cream. Add eggs one at a time, blending well after each addition. Mix in anise oil. Add flour mixture. Using a wooden spoon, mix into a soft dough.

4. Form dough into 2 12-inch-long by ½-inch thick loaves. Place on a greased cookie sheet and bake for 15 to 20 minutes, until light golden brown. Remove from oven and let cool.

5. Cut loaves diagonally into 1-inch-thick slices and place cut side down on cookie sheet. Return to oven and bake for about 5 minutes, until lightly toasted and dry.

Makes 24 cookies

COOK'S NOTES

ILLINOIS SUGAR COOKIES

FIRST LADY OF ILLINOIS BRENDA EDGAR • MARSHALL FIELD'S

"The Illinois Sugar Cookie recipe is an Edgar family favorite. It's become a traditional treat at the Executive Mansion. I hope you will enjoy sharing them with your family."

COOKIES

> 3 cups all-purpose flour
> 1 teaspoon cream of tartar
> ½ teaspoon baking soda
> ¼ teaspoon salt
> 1¼ cups (2½ sticks) butter or margarine,
>   at room temperature
> 1 cup granulated sugar
> 2 large eggs
> 3 tablespoons milk
> 1 teaspoon vanilla extract

FROSTING

> 5 tablespoons plus 1 teaspoon butter or margarine,
>   at room temperature
> 4½ cups confectioners' sugar, sifted
> ¼ cup milk
> ½ tablespoon vanilla extract
> ¼ to ½ teaspoon orange extract, ¼ teaspoon peppermint
>   extract, or ¼ teaspoon almond extract, if desired

1. Preheat oven to 375°F.

2. Make the cookies. In a medium bowl, stir together flour, cream of tartar, baking soda, and salt. Set aside.

3. Place butter or margarine in a large bowl. Using an electric mixer on medium speed, cream for 30 seconds. Add granulated sugar and beat until mixture is fluffy. Beat in eggs, milk, and vanilla until well combined. Add dry ingredients and beat just until thoroughly mixed.

4. Drop dough by teaspoonfuls onto ungreased cookie sheets, leaving 1 inch between cookies. Bake for 9 to 11 minutes, until edges of cookies are golden brown. Place on cooling racks to cool.

5. Make the frosting. Place butter or margarine in a small bowl. Using an electric mixer on medium speed, beat until fluffy. Beating constantly, gradually add 2 cups of the confectioners' sugar. Beat until smooth. Gradually beat in milk and vanilla. If desired, beat in extract. Slowly beat in remaining 2½ cups confectioners' sugar (beat in additional milk if frosting becomes too thick to spread). Spread frosting on cooled cookies.

Makes about 192 bite-sized cookies

COOK'S NOTES

HUNGARIAN TWISTS

EILEEN SULLIVAN • DAYTON'S

"I received this recipe from my close friend and neighbor Jan Gauger, who moved to Minnesota from Philadelphia. Over the past 20 years this recipe emigrated from her house, across the street, and up our driveway as my family demanded 'Jan's twists.' Baking them always reminds me of our friendship and of watching our kids running back and forth between our houses."

4 cups all-purpose flour
1 teaspoon salt
1 cup (2 sticks) butter or margarine, cut into pieces,
    at room temperature, plus 3 tablespoons, melted
1 ¼-ounce envelope active dry yeast
¼ cup warm water (105°F to 115°F)
¾ cup buttermilk
1 teaspoon vanilla extract
2 large eggs
¾ cup sugar
¾ teaspoon ground cinnamon

1. In a large mixing bowl, combine flour and salt. Using a pastry blender, cut 1 cup butter or margarine into flour mixture until mixture resembles coarse meal (as if making a piecrust).

2. In a mixing bowl, dissolve yeast in warm water. Stir in buttermilk and vanilla. Pour into flour mixture and stir. By hand, knead in eggs one at a time until dough is smooth. Cover and refrigerate for at least 2 hours.

3. Preheat oven to 350°F.

4. In a bowl, mix together sugar and cinnamon.

5. On a lightly floured work surface divide dough into 3 balls. Roll one ball out into a ¼-inch-thick oblong shape. Brush with 1 tablespoon melted butter. Sprinkle with about ¼ cup sugar-cinnamon mixture. Fold dough in half crosswise. Gently roll out to about 9″ × 12″. Cut in half lengthwise. Cut each half into 9 1-inch-wide strips. Twist each strip twice and place on ungreased cookie sheets. Repeat process for remainder of dough.

6. Bake until golden brown (about 20 minutes). Transfer to cooling racks to cool.

Makes 54 twists

COOK'S NOTES

GLAZED APPLE COOKIES

SHIRLEY MICHAELSON • DAYTON'S

"Everyone loves these cookies. They freeze very well, too."

COOKIES

1 cup vegetable oil
3 cups packed light brown sugar
1 teaspoon salt
2 teaspoons ground cinnamon
1 teaspoon ground nutmeg
½ teaspoon ground cloves
2 large eggs
2 teaspoons baking soda
5 cups all-purpose flour
½ cup milk
4 cups peeled, cored, and chopped
    McIntosh apples (4 to 5 apples)
½ cup dark raisins
½ cup chopped walnuts

GLAZE

2 cups confectioners' sugar
1 teaspoon vanilla extract
3 tablespoons hot milk
2 tablespoons butter

1. Preheat oven to 400°F.

2. Make the cookies. In a very large mixing bowl, combine oil, brown sugar, salt, spices, and eggs. Beat until well blended. Add baking soda, flour, milk, apples, raisins, and nuts. Mix thoroughly until flour has been well incorporated.

3. Using a generous 2 tablespoons batter for each, drop batter onto 4 lightly greased cookie sheets, leaving 3 inches between cookies. Bake for 10 to 12 minutes, until cookies are lightly browned and firm to the touch. Let cookies cool on the sheets for 2 minutes. Transfer to cooling racks.

4. Make the glaze. In a bowl, combine all ingredients. Stir until smooth. Spread glaze over warm cookies.

Makes 4 to 5 dozen cookies

COOK'S NOTES

CARRICKFERGUS SHORTBREAD

SARAH NAIRN • DAYTON'S

"My husband is from Carrickfergus, Northern Ireland. When we were first married and living in England, I tried several different recipes for shortbread, his favorite treat with tea. After many batches that were too dry, too sweet, too crumbly, too thick, I hit upon the perfect recipe. Now the only request from my husband is 'Don't change it!'"

> 5½ cups all-purpose flour
> ½ cup cornstarch
> 1 teaspoon salt
> 3 cups (6 sticks) butter, at room temperature
> 1½ cups sugar plus additional to sprinkle on top
> 1 teaspoon vanilla extract

1. Preheat oven to 350°F.

2. In a large bowl, combine flour, cornstarch, and salt. Set aside.

3. Place butter and sugar in another large bowl. Using an electric mixer at medium speed, cream until fluffy. Add flour mixture and mix at low speed until thoroughly incorporated. Mix in vanilla.

4. Press dough into an ungreased 12″ × 18″ baking sheet. Using the tines of a fork, prick surface of dough all over. Sprinkle lightly with sugar.

5. Bake for 30 minutes, until edges of shortbread just begin to brown. Remove from oven. Using a sharp knife, score into 48 1½″ × 3″ fingers. Return to oven, turn off heat, and let cool for 2 to 3 hours. Store in airtight tins.

Makes 48 cookies

GRANDMA'S OATMEAL FUDGE DROP COOKIES

PATTY MILLER • HUDSON'S

This recipe is from the collection of Mary Helen Kennedy. Patty writes, "Every year Mom would make up a batch of these cookies for all of our school-teachers, who loved them. No matter how bare our cupboards were, all of the ingredients needed to prepare these were always there. Every time I make these for my own children, I feel as if I'm right back in my mom's kitchen. I'm passing this recipe on to every grandchild, along with a little story about the recipe's place in our family history."

> 2 cups sugar
> ½ cup (1 stick) butter or margarine
> ½ cup milk
> ½ cup unsweetened cocoa powder
> 3 cups rolled oats
> ⅓ cup creamy peanut butter
> 2 teaspoons vanilla extract

1. In a saucepan, combine sugar, butter, milk, and cocoa. Bring to a boil over medium-high heat. Cook, stirring frequently, for 4 minutes. Remove from heat. Add oats, peanut butter, and vanilla. Mix until combined.

2. Line 2 cookie sheets with aluminum foil. Drop level tablespoons onto foil. Refrigerate until set.

Makes about 40 cookies

COOK'S NOTES

UNIMAGINABLE CHOCOLATE CHIP COOKIES

DARRON SCHMIT • DAYTON'S

"Grandma Schmit's kitchen was the most wonderful place imaginable. It was always filled with the aroma of some kind of treat or another. To this day, the smell of these cookies baking brings back memories of warmth and family. I share this recipe with you in memory of my Grandma Norma Schmit."

> 1 cup (2 sticks) butter, at room temperature
> 1 cup granulated sugar
> 1 cup packed light brown sugar
> 1 large egg
> ¾ cup vegetable oil
> 2 tablespoons milk
> 1 teaspoon vanilla extract
> 3½ cups all-purpose flour
> 1 teaspoon cream of tartar
> 1 teaspoon baking soda
> Dash salt
> 1 12-ounce bag (2 cups) semisweet chocolate chips
> ¾ cup chopped pecans

1. Preheat oven to 350°F.

2. Place butter and sugars in a large bowl. Using an electric mixer at medium speed, cream. Beat in egg. Continue to beat until mixture is fluffy. Beat in oil, milk, and vanilla.

3. In a large bowl, whisk together flour, cream of tartar, baking soda, and salt. Add to butter mixture. Using a wooden spoon, mix together. Fold in chocolate chips and nuts.

4. Using 2 tablespoons dough for each, drop dough onto ungreased cookie sheets, leaving 2 inches space between cookies. Bake for about 10 minutes, until firm. Transfer cookies to cooling racks and let cool.

Makes about 36 cookies

COOK'S NOTES

AUNT GAIL'S BROWNIES

GAIL SHAW • MARSHALL FIELD'S

"This is a favorite recipe of my family. I'm always asked to bring these brownies to any family function whether it's my side of the family or my husband's. That makes me feel very special."

BROWNIES

1½ cups all-purpose flour
1 teaspoon salt
1 teaspoon baking powder
4 1-ounce squares unsweetened chocolate
⅔ cup vegetable oil
2 cups granulated sugar
4 eggs, beaten
1 cup chopped pecans

FROSTING

1 1-ounce square unsweetened chocolate
2 tablespoons butter, melted
1 teaspoon vanilla extract
Dash salt
3 tablespoons milk
1½ to 2 cups confectioners' sugar

1. Preheat oven to 350°F.

2. Make the brownies. In a large bowl, sift together flour, salt, and baking powder. Set aside.

3. In the top of a double boiler over hot (not boiling) water or in a microwave oven, melt chocolate. Transfer to a large bowl. Stir in oil, granulated sugar, eggs, and nuts. Stir in flour mixture. Mix well.

4. Pour batter into a greased and floured 9″ × 13″ pan and bake for 25 to 35 minutes, until a toothpick inserted in center comes out clean. Remove from oven and let cool in pan on a cooling rack before frosting.

5. Make the frosting. In the top of a double boiler over hot (not boiling) water or in a microwave oven, melt chocolate. Transfer to a medium bowl. Add butter, vanilla, salt, and milk and blend well. Continuing to mix, gradually add confectioners' sugar until desired consistency is reached. Spread frosting over cool brownies. Cut into serving-size squares.

Makes about 20 brownies

COOK'S NOTES

PEANUT BARS

TIM PEPERA • DAYTON'S

"When I was young, my grandmother would always offer these as a special treat whenever we visited her."

> 2 cups granulated sugar
> 2 cups cake flour
> 2 teaspoons baking powder
> ¼ teaspoon salt
> 1 cup milk
> 6 large egg whites, at room temperature
> 1 teaspoon vanilla extract
> 3 cups (18 ounces) ground unsalted blanched peanuts
> 2 cups confectioners' sugar
> ½ cup heavy cream

1. Preheat oven to 350°F.

2. In a large mixing bowl, sift together granulated sugar, flour, baking powder, and salt.

3. In a small saucepan, scald milk over medium heat (until bubbles begin to form around the edge). Fold milk into sugar mixture.

4. Place egg whites in a large bowl. Using an electric mixer at medium speed, beat egg whites until very stiff but not dry. Beat in vanilla. Fold in flour-milk mixture.

5. Place batter in a greased 9″ × 13″ baking pan and bake for 25 to 30 minutes, until a toothpick inserted in center of cake comes out clean and cake begins to pull away from sides of pan. Transfer pan to a cooling rack and let cool for about 2 hours. Cut into generous 2-inch squares.

6. Place peanuts in a wide, shallow dish. In a separate bowl, combine confectioners' sugar and cream. Using a fork, mix thoroughly. Frost the top and sides of each bar. Roll each in ground nuts.

Makes 24 bars

COOK'S NOTES

GRANDMA TRACY'S LEMON SLICES

RENEE TRACY • MARSHALL FIELD'S

"I received this recipe from my mother-in-law about 15 years ago. It's perfect for a large group—everyone loves it, and it's a delicious ending to a great meal."

> 3 cups crushed vanilla wafers
> ½ cup (1 stick) butter or margarine, melted
> 1 8-ounce package cream cheese, at room temperature
> 1 cup confectioners' sugar
> 4 to 5 teaspoons milk
> 1 teaspoon vanilla extract
> 2 2.9-ounce packages lemon pie filling (do not use instant)
> 1 cup granulated sugar
> ½ cup warm water
> 4 large egg yolks
> 1 quart cold water
> 1 cup heavy cream, whipped

1. Preheat oven to 375°F.

2. In a bowl, combine wafers and butter or margarine. Press evenly into a lightly greased 11″ × 15″ baking sheet and bake until firm (about 8 minutes). Remove from oven and let cool on a cooling rack.

3. In a medium bowl, combine cream cheese, confectioners' sugar, and milk. Using a wooden spoon, mix until smooth and spreadable. Stir in vanilla. Spread mixture over cooled crust.

4. In a large saucepan, combine pie filling, granulated sugar, warm water, and egg yolks. Mix well. Stir in cold water. Bring to a rolling boil over medium heat, stirring constantly. Remove from heat and let cool for 5 minutes, stirring every 1½ to 2 minutes. Pour over cream cheese mixture.

5. Cover with plastic wrap and refrigerate for at least 2 hours. Top with a thin layer of whipped cream and cut into serving-size slices.

Makes 24 to 30 slices

COOK'S NOTES

CARAMEL HEAVENLIES

DIANA BARTOLOTTA • HUDSON'S

"This recipe is delightful. It's so different from the usual cookie—the perfect treat for the holidays."

12 whole graham crackers (5" × 2½" crackers)
2 cups miniature marshmallows
¾ cup (1½ sticks) butter or margarine
¾ cup packed dark brown sugar
1 teaspoon ground cinnamon
1 teaspoon vanilla extract
1 cup (about 6 ounces) sliced blanched almonds
    or chopped walnuts
1 cup flaked sweetened coconut

1. Preheat oven to 350°F.

2. Arrange graham crackers in a single layer in a 15½" × 10" baking sheet. Sprinkle with marshmallows.

3. In a medium saucepan, combine butter, brown sugar, and cinnamon. Cook over medium heat, stirring constantly, until sugar has dissolved (3 to 5 minutes). Remove from heat and stir in vanilla. Spoon mixture evenly over marshmallows. Sprinkle with nuts and coconut.

4. Bake for 12 to 14 minutes, until lightly browned. Transfer pan to a cooling rack and let cool. Cut into 2½-inch squares.

Makes 24 squares

COOK'S NOTES

GREAT AUNT MARY'S NUT ROLLS

ELLEN R. ZEHNDER • HUDSON'S

"My great aunt Mary used to make these when I was younger. I loved them so much, she gave me the recipe."

> 1 cup (2 sticks) butter or margarine, at room temperature
> 1 8-ounce package cream cheese, at room temperature
> 2½ cups all-purpose flour
> 1½ cups (about 9 ounces) ground walnuts
> 1 cup sugar
> ¼ cup milk
> 1 large egg, beaten

1. Place butter and cream cheese in a large bowl. Using an electric mixer at medium speed, cream. Mix in flour until incorporated. Shape dough into a 5-inch square 2 inches thick. Refrigerate for 1 hour.

2. In a bowl, combine walnuts, sugar, and milk. Using a fork, mix into a paste.

3. Cut dough into 5 1-inch-wide strips. Place 1 strip on a lightly floured work surface and roll out as thin as possible into a 10-inch square. Cut dough into 16 2½-inch squares. Spread a scant teaspoon of the walnut mixture on each square. Roll squares up jelly-roll style and place on 3 greased cookie sheets. Repeat process for remaining dough strips.

4. Brush rolls with beaten egg. Bake for 22 to 25 minutes, until golden brown. Transfer to cooling racks and let cool.

Makes 80 nut rolls

COOK'S NOTES

BAKLAVA

ERTUGRUL TUZCU • DAYTON'S

"This is a famous Turkish delicacy. I learned how to make it by watching my grandmother 30 years ago. Now it's a Tuzcu family favorite."

1 16-ounce package phyllo dough
2 cups sugar
1 cup water
1 tablespoon grated lemon zest
1 tablespoon lemon juice
½ to ¾ cup (1 to 1½ sticks) unsalted butter, melted
2 cups (about 8 ounces) finely chopped walnuts
2 tablespoons ground cinnamon

1. Thaw phyllo dough according to package directions.

2. In a saucepan, combine sugar, water, lemon zest, and lemon juice. Bring to a full boil and boil for 2 minutes. Set syrup aside to cool.

3. Lay a sheet of phyllo in a buttered 12″ × 18″ jelly-roll pan and brush sheet with melted butter. Repeat process with 9 more sheets of phyllo. Spread walnuts in an even layer over top sheet. Sprinkle with cinnamon. Add remaining phyllo sheets, brushing melted butter over each. Using a serrated knife, trim dough at edges. Freeze for 15 minutes.

4. Preheat oven to 350°F.

5. Using a serrated knife, score top of dough 5 times lengthwise, then 8 times on the diagonal to make diamond shapes. Bake for 30 minutes, until golden. Immediately pour syrup evenly over baklava. Let cool for at least 30 minutes before serving.

Makes about 38 pieces

COOK'S NOTES

RASPBERRY TRIFLE

LIZ FLYNN • DAYTON'S

"There are as many trifle recipes as there are cooks' imaginations. I thought it would be fun to create my own version, and this is the delicious result."

> 2 3-ounce packages instant vanilla pudding
> 2 cups whipping cream
> 1 1-pound loaf pound cake
> 1 12-ounce jar seedless raspberry jam
> 2 10-ounce packages frozen raspberries with syrup, thawed
> 1 8-ounce container fresh raspberries

1. Prepare pudding per package directions.

2. Place cream in a bowl. Using an electric mixer at high speed, whip until soft peaks form.

3. Cut pound cake into ¼-inch-thick slices. Spread about ½ tablespoon jam evenly on one side of each slice.

4. Assemble the trifle. Spread a third of the pudding on the bottom of a trifle bowl. Top with a third of the pound cake slices, jam side down. Top with a third of the thawed berries and a third of their syrup. Top with a third of the whipped cream. Repeat process twice. Sprinkle fresh berries on top.

Serves 12 to 15

COOK'S NOTES

BREAD PUDDING with VANILLA SAUCE

ANNE SIMONS • HUDSON'S

"My husband, Henry, and I were once interviewed by a reporter from the Detroit Free Press. The reporter asked my husband what he liked best about my cooking, and to my surprise, he said that bread pudding was his favorite dessert."

PUDDING

15 slices white bread, cut into 1-inch cubes
½ cup (1 stick) butter, melted
6 large eggs
1 quart milk
1¼ cups sugar
1 teaspoon vanilla extract
1 cup dark raisins

VANILLA SAUCE

4 large egg yolks
1 tablespoon all-purpose flour
2 teaspoons vanilla extract
Pinch salt
2 cups heavy cream
½ cup sugar
1 scoop vanilla ice cream

COOK'S NOTES

1. Preheat oven to 450°F.

2. Make the pudding. On a large baking sheet, arrange bread cubes in a single layer. Bake for about 7 minutes, until lightly toasted. Remove from oven and let cool. Reduce oven temperature to 350°F.

3. Arrange bread in the bottom of a shallow 2½-quart baking dish. Drizzle with melted butter.

4. In a large mixing bowl, combine eggs, milk, sugar, and vanilla. Whisk until smooth. Stir in raisins. Pour mixture over bread and bake for 40 to 45 minutes, until mixture is set in center (gently shake the pan to determine if center is set). Remove from oven and let cool on a cooling rack.

5. Make the sauce. In a mixing bowl, combine egg yolks, flour, vanilla, and salt. Whisk lightly.

6. In a saucepan, combine cream and sugar. Cook over medium heat just until bubbles begin to form around the edge of the pan (about 3 minutes). Remove from heat and slowly whisk 1 cup sugar mixture into egg mixture. Whisk mixture back into pan. Cook over low heat for about 2 minutes, stirring constantly, until thickened. Remove from heat and stir in ice cream. Strain sauce through a sieve if necessary. Serve over warm or chilled pudding.

Serves 12

COOK'S NOTES

RICE PUDDING

Beverly Kabakoff Adilman • Marshall Field's

"The first time I made dinner for my husband-to-be, he asked for his favorite dessert: rice pudding. I'd never made it before, but, because I loved him (and I loved a good challenge), I honored the request. The pudding I created turned out to be so great that it led to a proposal. To this day, I don't know if it's me or my pudding that keeps our marriage together."

⅔ cup long-grain white rice
2¼ cups water
⅔ cup sugar
2¼ teaspoons cornstarch
½ teaspoon salt
2⅔ cups half-and-half

2 tablespoons butter
1¼ teaspoons vanilla extract
4 large egg yolks
Garnish: ground cinnamon or
    ground nutmeg

1. In a medium saucepan, bring rice and water to a boil over medium heat. Cover, reduce heat to low, and simmer for 30 to 35 minutes, until rice is tender and most of the water has been absorbed. Remove from heat.

2. In a bowl, combine sugar, cornstarch, and salt. Stir into rice. Stir in half-and-half. Bring to a boil over medium heat, stirring constantly. Boil for 1 minute. Remove from heat and stir in butter and vanilla.

3. In a small bowl, lightly beat egg yolks. Gradually stir in 1 cup hot rice mixture. Stir combination back into pan. Cook over medium heat, stirring often, just until pudding begins to bubble (3 to 5 minutes).

4. Serve pudding warm or cold. Garnish with ground cinnamon or ground nutmeg.

Serves 6

COOK'S NOTES

CHARLOTTE RUSSE

JOYCE OSTERGREN • DAYTON'S

"This recipe is over 100 years old. Prepared for special occasions, including birthdays, it is always the main event of any meal."

2½ tablespoons (2½ ¼-ounce packets) unflavored gelatin
½ cup cold water
3 cups milk
4 large eggs, lightly beaten
1½ cups sugar
Pinch salt

1 8-inch angel food cake, sliced thin
1 quart heavy cream, whipped
2 1-ounce squares semisweet chocolate, melted
2 teaspoons vanilla extract
1½ teaspoons peppermint extract

1. In a small bowl, mix gelatin and water. Stir to dissolve gelatin and set aside.

2. In a medium saucepan, combine milk, eggs, sugar, and salt. Cook over low heat for 5 to 7 minutes, stirring occasionally, until mixture is thick enough to coat the back of a spoon. Remove from heat and stir in gelatin mixture. Let cool.

3. While custard is cooling, line bottom and sides of a very large serving bowl with cake slices. When custard is cool and has begun to set, fold in whipped cream. Divide evenly between 2 bowls. In one bowl, stir in melted chocolate and vanilla. Pour over cake. In the other bowl, stir in peppermint. Pour over cake. Cover and refrigerate for 4 hours.

Serves 16

COOK'S NOTES

GRANDMA NAT'S CARAMELS

DEBORAH SCHMITZ • MARSHALL FIELD'S

"This recipe has been in our family for generations, handed down to family members by my grandma Nat. We prepare these caramels during the Christmas season—they're a favorite of friends and family, and I would like to share them with you."

2 cups sugar
1 cup light corn syrup
1 quart heavy cream
1 teaspoon vanilla extract

1. Butter an 8-inch-square baking pan and set aside.

2. In a large kettle (at least 4 quarts), combine sugar, corn syrup, and 1⅓ cups cream. Cook over medium-high heat, stirring gently but almost constantly (to keep mixture from scorching or sticking to the bottom of the pan) until mixture reaches a temperature of 240°F on a candy thermometer (about 30 minutes).

3. In a slow stream, add another 1⅓ cups cream. Cook, stirring constantly, until mixture again reaches a temperature of 240°F. Repeat process. (Steps 2 and 3 will take about 1¼ hours to complete.)

4. Stir in vanilla. Immediately pour caramel into baking pan. Place on a cooling rack and let cool for at least 1 hour. Refrigerate until firm (about 2 hours) and cut into 1-inch squares. Wrap each caramel individually in wax paper.

Makes 64 caramels

Contributors

Beverly Kabakoff Adilman
Leslie Alexopoulos
Karen Jane Altman
Cheryl Anderson
Jeanette Anderson
Laurel Anthony
The Honorable Dennis Archer, Mayor, City of Detroit, and The Honorable Trudy Duncombe Archer, Judge, 36th District Court
Bernice Bambulis
Diana Bartolotta
Cindy Baubie
Barbara Bayley
Minneapolis Mayor Sharon Sayles Belton
Pamela Degener Benz
Beverly Berkenbilt
Sally Blair
Pam Boe

Jan Bohannon
Suzanne Bosserd
Mary Bradley
Mary C. Braun
Joan Bussen
Edith Cahn
Maureen Caliman
Kaye Campbell
Pamela Cavanaugh
Carole Chandler
Mary Ann Cheng
Tina Chiappa
Patricia Chipman
Arlene Chisholm
Colleen M. Chmelko
Christi Clancy
St. Paul Mayor Norm Coleman and Laurie Coleman
Roseann Corallo
Alyce Cueller
Madlyn Daniel
Nancy Darbut
Maria DeLuca
Joan Deutsch
Susan A. Diehl

Eileen Drew
Barbara A. Duchene
Donna V. Duffield
Cathy Dunn
Brenda Edgar, First Lady of Illinois
Debra J. Edwards
Dorothy Falkenberg
Liz Flynn
Elizabeth Forster
Sue Friedman
Amy M. Gable
Sheila Gershman
Sandra Hamlin
Bridget Haubold
Shellie Herman
Kathie Hilton
Ginny Grafitti Hodina
Joan Hodsdon
Vicki Holtan
Sheila Horst
Cathy Horvath
Christopher Howse
Del Hulett
Wayne A. Hunt

Alice Jacobson
Mrs. Jeane Jenson
Diane M. Johnson
Marlys Johnson
Myrna Johnson
Sally Johnson
Elaine Jorgensen
Susan Keldani
Laurie King
Karen Kletter
Marlene A. Konsdorf
Sandra Kort
Susan Kramer
Ellen Liner Lasner
Lana Lie
Lois F. Lindquist
Lia LoChirco
Dr. John S. Long
Joan H. Lowenstein
Ed Lowenstern
Estelle Makrouer
Celia Manlove
Diana Luna Martinez
Ursula Maurer
Patti McEachron
Louise McNamara

Carol Menz
Shirley Michaelson
Patty Miller
Shirley Moore
Thelma Moore
Margaret M. Mourad
Joyce Mundahl
Jenifer Murray
Bonnie Nagle
Sarah Nairn
Stephanie Nankervis
Linda Newsome
Lisa Novak
Julianne Nyberg
Mary Jane O'Connell
Ayako Olsson
Joyce Ostergren

Rosalyn H. Pachter
Audrey E. Paul
Joyce Peltz
Josephine Pennucci
Tim Pepera
Mary Piper
Donna Portelli
Laurie Ann Redlowsk
Kathryn Reutzel
Marie Rizzio
Mareen L. Roach
Deb Roeser
Gabrielle
    Sappenfield
Pam Schmidt
Darron Schmit
Deborah Schmitz

Gail Shaw
Beverly J. Sherman
Kari Siegel
Anne Simons
Marilyn Smith
Rose E. Snider
Eileen Sullivan
Phyllis O. Sutcliffe
Millicent Sutherland
Linda Swanson
Karin Marya Tansek,
    M.D.
Marlene Temple
Joan and Terri
    Tiersky
Renee Tracy
Ertugrul Tuzcu

Margaret Van Bergen
Ruth Vanden Bosch
Marilyn Vandermark
Karen Vander Wagen
James A. Vitek
Jeanne DeWolfe
    Walters
Leslie Ward
Libby Franco Weil
Doris V. Wicks
Sharalee Wilson and
    Arline Carter
Jane M. Workman
Ellen R. Zehnder

INDEX